Shelter Amongst the Shadows

REFLECTIONS UPON SUCCOS AND MEGILLAS KOHELES

Moshe M. Eisemann

2ⁿᵈ Revised Edition, © Moshe M. Eisemann, 2005
1ˢᵗ Edition Published 1998

All rights reserved under international copyright conventions.
No part of this book maybe reproduced or utilized in any form
or by any means, electronic or mechanical, including photocopying,
recording, or by any information storage and retrieval system,
without permission in writing from the publisher:

Rabbi Moshe M. Eisemann
403 Yeshiva Lane, Apt 1B
Baltimore, MD 21208
410-484-7396
www.yeshivakishiniev.org

Managing Editor: Nama Frenkel
Copy Editor: Yacov Dovid Shulman
Design and typesetting: Jerusalem Typesetting, www.jerusalemtype.com

ISBN: 0-9769161-2-6

Distributed by:
Feldheim Publishers
POB 35002, Jerusalem, Israel 91350
200 Airport Executive Park, Nanuet, NY, 10954
www.feldheim.com

Printed in the US and UK by www.lightingpress.com

Contents

Preface

THIS SMALL COLLECTION of essays does not pretend to be a full-fledged commentary on *Koheles*. The range of topics is in no sense exhaustive, and the subjects with which the essays deal could lend themselves to much deeper and much more comprehensive analysis. So this book is only a tiny sampling from a vast pool of potential.

Nevertheless, *Shelter Amongst the Shadows* serves a purpose; perhaps even an important one. By a careful reading of the text it attempts to plumb some aspects of King Solomon's wisdom at the level of *p'shat*—the straightforward meaning. It really does no more than to seek to understand some of the constantly recurring key words which, by their repeated use, serve to sharpen the thrust of the megillah's teaching, and to give it direction and nuance. In pursuing this modest goal, it seeks to lay bare some of the surface truths that a more cursory reading might well miss.

When our Sages decided to have *Koheles* read on Succos, they clearly wanted to establish a symbiotic relationship between the two. The profound lessons of the megillah would animate our experience of the holiday and, embraced in the sacred space of our *succah*, we would become sensitized to messages and meanings which at other times in other circumstances would simply pass us by.

But for all this to take place, we need to have at least a surface understanding of the book.

Koheles is particularly difficult to learn. Whenever we study TaNaCH we turn instinctively to Rashi for help in understanding the basic meaning of the material. We have been raised on his assertions, appearing frequently in the Chumash commentary, that his aim is to present the simplest, clearest interpretation of each verse, and we take for granted that this is also his purpose in the NaCH commentary. However, frequently this is simply not the case.

It is not my intention in the present context to make blanket judgments or assumptions about the principles that guided Rashi in his commentary to NaCH. Even if one were to assume that, after the passage of centuries, it would be possible to arrive at a reasonable hypothesis, this could only be done by dint of a painstaking analysis of the entire corpus, an undertaking that lies far beyond my competence.

However, a much more modest goal is very much within our reach. We can study Rashi to *Koheles* carefully and lovingly, and find that very frequently he offers only midrashic material, leaving the discovery of the simple meaning of the text in all its complexities to the reader.[1]

Over the centuries, many commentators have risen to this challenge. A glance at even a standard edition of TaNaCH will reveal the wide range of possibilities that are embedded in the text.

And so we have tried to read the megillah carefully and thoughtfully to see what we could see, to learn what we could learn.

We have concentrated on themes that would reveal the megillah's affinity with the holiday of Succos. For this we needed to make assumptions about Succos and about *Koheles*. These are as follows: We assume that Succos celebrates the ordinary life: eating, sleeping and just spending time, provided that it takes place away from the searing physicality of the sun, within the sacred shadow of the *succah*.[2] This, precisely, appears also to be the message of *Koheles*. It is a lyric affirmation of this-worldly life as long as it is not weighted by the cloying futility that drains all activity undertaken *under the sun* of its lilt and its music.

Succos proclaims, and *Koheles* joyfully affirms, that this wonderful world which God has given us, the society of men in which he has planted us, we ourselves with all our faults and blemishes, can all play our role, happily and productively, if we just learn how to do it right.

The sun, standing for all that is physical in our world, is both the villain and hero of our megillah. Let it control you, and the entire edifice which God so lovingly fashioned during the six days of creation, even the Shabbos through which He breathed meaning into it, disintegrates into so much dross. That, as our Sages teach us, is the meaning of the seven pronouncements of *vanity* with which the megillah opens. But get out from under the sun's destructive rays, move into the shade cast by the *s'chach*, the thatch roof, of your *succah*, or the *yir'as shomayim* your daily life as taught in *Koheles*, and the sun becomes *a benign sun carrying healing in its rays* (*Malachi* 3:20).

*   *   *

As an appropriate ending to this Preface we will analyze more closely the *Malachi* passage in which the above verse occurs. In three short sentences, it summarizes the entire thesis that forms the backbone of our small book.

16. ‫אז נדברו יראי ה' איש את רעהו ...‬
Then those who fear Hashem spoke to one another ...

17. ‫... וחמלתי עליהם כאשר יחמל איש על בנו העבד אתו.‬
And I will have mercy on them as a father has mercy upon a son who serves him.

18.   ושבתם וראיתם בין צדיק לרשע בין עבד אלהים לאשר
לא עבדו.

Then you will return and see the difference between the righteous and the wicked, between those who serve God and those who do not serve Him.

19.   כי הנה היום בא בער כתנור והיו כל זדים ... קש ולהט אתם
היום הבא ...

For behold the day is coming burning like an oven, when all the wicked ... will be like straw and the coming day will consume them.

20.   וזרחה לכם יראי שמי שמש צדקה ומרפא בכנפיה ויצאתם
ופשתם כעגלי מרבק.

But for you who fear My Name a benign sun with healing in its rays will shine, and you will spread out and wax corpulent like calves being fattened in the stall.

22.   זכרו תורת משה עבדי ...

Remember the Torah of My servant Moshe ...

Let us listen carefully. These are the final words of the very last of the prophets. What was said now would have to last us through the dark and lonesome centuries of heavy, unbroken silence.

What would be the final message which God would want to send along with us? What would be able to sustain us during the dreadful track through the valley of our estrangement?

Here it is. The fear of God, and its active mode, service, would see us through.

The rigors of exile will serve as a crucible. They will build and they will break. There will be those who serve God and those who do not. There will be the loyal and the faithless. There will be those who stand proudly straight as they stoop to bear the yoke of bondage, and there will be the craven whose spine buckles under the weight.

And a day will come. Throughout the terrors of the seem-ingly endless night we are to remember that. Dawn is go-ing to break. The long road, littered with so many shattered hopes, will lead us where we need to go. A day will come. The sun will rise. And it will be a sun like no other that we have known. It will carry vengeance and benevolence in its glow. It will consume those who allowed themselves to be seduced by its allures. They lived their lives *under the sun;* they are to learn that unbridled physicality is just a synonym for destruction.

But there will be others, those who fear Hashem, those who learned well the lesson which Koheles struggles to teach us. They were *the ones who see the sun,* the ones who refused to subordinate themselves to the sun and all its blandish-ments. They stood on the outside—never beneath—observ-ing, judging, weighing. They knew what to accept and what to reject. For them the sun was always good, it's light always sweet (11:7). On that dreadful day it will continue to smile upon them.

But there is more, much more. What are we to make of the final phrase in verse 20: *And you will spread out and wax corpulent as the calves being fattened in the stall?* Is that really what we want? Is that our vision of the ideal life after history will have run its course?

The answer appears to be yes. The phrase, in its own par-ticularly vivid imagery, does not, after all, promise anything different than does the Torah, in all its assurances that the righteously lived life will be rewarded by all the bounties that the earth has to offer. We are human; we have physical needs and, if we will but admit it, crave their gratification. If the formulation sounds coarse and indelicate to our ears, it is because we tend to function in an *under the sun* mode, one in which the implications are indeed revolting. If we could only be the kind of people for whom the sun is *a benign sun with healing in its rays,* then Malachi's promise would not appear at all inappropriate. God gave us the world, and He gave it to us to enjoy.

It is as we have said. The *Malachi* passage encapsulates the message of *Koheles* as we understand it. We can truly assert that the ideal towards which the megillah wants to guide and goad us can be summed up in this one verse so full of understanding, so full of promise:

וזרחה לכם יראי שמי שמש צדקה ומרפא בכנפיה
But for you who fear My Name a benign sun with healing in its rays will shine.

*   *   *

Having said all this, we must not lose sight of the fact that the passage that we have now analyzed is not the prophet's absolutely final word. It is the penultimate section, not the last.

His final exhortation, the very last thought with which he sends us on our way, is this: *Remember the Torah of Moses, My servant ….* When all has been said, when all has been done, there is only one path that can guarantee that we will never stray from the protective shadow of the fear of heaven. We must learn, learn and then learn some more. There is nothing else. There really, really is nothing else.

Let us recall that even Succos culminates with Simchas Torah. That is an awesome thought and we need to ponder a little more about its implications. Of this, more in the final essay of our book.

KUZARI: …Who, from the Jewish perspective, would be considered a true servant of God …?

SAGE: Certainly not a hermit who shuns society. A true servant of God would never consider life, God's greatest gift, a burden. It is to be savored, each additional moment thought of as a precious boon, because it is a sure path to the world-to-come. Each fleeting moment can yield eternity.

… For most people a life of asceticism would be self defeating. They would crave all those legitimate experiences for which nature endowed them. Sounds and sights, the company of friends, the daily challenge of living and of making a living would all clamor for attention. We want to eat, to drink and to live normal married lives. We want to make money, to have decent homes, to lend a hand to the needy and to support Torah scholars with our bounty. A life of exaggerated austerity will simply backfire. It will drive a wedge between the would-be hermit and God, rather than bring them closer together. Instead of making him feel holy, it will make him bitter because of all that he has missed.

KUZARI: If asceticism is not the defining characteristic of piety, what then would mark a person as pious?

SAGE: It is not a matter of self-denial but of prudence and discipline. Much like a wise ruler who understands his subjects and makes the best use of his resources, the pious person will know the measure of his body's needs and neither withhold from it what is necessary nor indulge it in what is not. His respect and discretion will be rewarded by loyal performance. Eyes, ears, hands and feet, the heart, the mind and the mouth, all will jump to his service as he calls upon them. Unencumbered by constant struggle with a recalcitrant physicality, he can turn his attention to living a full religious life …

(This is a loose translation of the beginning of the third section of *The Kuzari* by Reb Yehudah HaLevi.)

THE DAY

Shelter in the Shade

S TRICTLY SPEAKING, Yom Kippur and Succos respectively belong to different sets. The concepts of the Days of Awe and the three pilgrim festivals are too familiar to require much analysis in the present context. So it really would be possible to view the proximity of these two celebrations to one another as simply accidental. There seems to be no natural flow from Yom Kippur to Succos. Yom Kippur is on the tenth of Tishrei and Succos on the fifteenth, and that is all there is to it.

It is possible, but Jewishly wrong. Not after all the caring and cleansing of Yom Kippur. Not after all that love.

It is inconceivable that Yom Kippur should simply be over and done with, and Succos just happens to come along. So it is not a coincidence. It has to happen. Fresh from Yom Kippur there is only one place to go, and that is into the *succah*.

Why? Because what we have gained on Yom Kippur is very, very precious. Because we the people, unsullied once more and receptive to holiness, are consummately precious. Yom Kippur makes us free[1] and freedom needs to be guarded jealously. Succos cradles us in its protective and nurturing embrace. It draws us out from under the searing sun and bids us come into the shade.

Let us analyze.

CANOPIES OF PEACE

It really is a process that we go through every night. After reciting the *Shema*, we meditate upon the implications of the Egyptian experience. We recognize God as our redeemer: *Blessed are You, Redeemer of Israel.* And immediately afterwards, we ask that *You spread over us Your canopy of peace*—literally, *Your succah of peace.*

Freedom, then, needs protection. There would be no point in taking us out of Egypt and then simply leaving us to our own devices. The first stop after we left Raamses was Succos. Our first entreaty after our nightly celebration of redemption is that God spread His protective Canopy of Peace over us.

And after Yom Kippur comes Succos.[2]

But we are still only at the beginning. We trust our new-found freedom to the *succah*. That is a given. But how does the *succah* do its job? In what way does the *succah* really help us?

In the context of Koheles, the answer is really very simple.

CASTING SHADOWS

Rashi to the first mishnah in Tractate *Succos* teaches us that the noun *succah* derives from the root *s'chach*, to cast a shade.[3] The *succah*, then, is a structure that, before all else, provides shade.

In Koheles, the villain is the sun:

מה יתרון לאדם בכל עמלו שיעמול תחת השמש

What advantage is there to a man in all his toil that
he engages in under the sun?

The sun in all its crass physical vitality, in the endless circularity of its motion (or perceived motion) rules over a world that comes as close to self-sufficiency as anything could possibly come. It is the focus of basic idolatry[4] for just this reason. Activities undertaken under its aegis (*under the sun*) are bereft of any connection to the Divine. They are *vanity* in all its pointless emptiness.

If after Yom Kippur we would remain *under the sun* (read: under the aegis of the sun), then the entire experience would have been an exercise in futility. We would be living a life of pure, crass, unsublimated physicality. What, in the end, would have been the point?

The *succah* tells us that it need not be so. Come into the shade, it calls out to us, and your eating, your everyday activities, even your sleeping, can be touched by the grace of sanctity.[5] Come into the shade and you can consolidate all that you gained on Yom Kippur. You need not jettison your normal life but need to make it holy. Learn how to do this for seven days and it will transform you and your life. You will become what you so desperately wanted to become on Yom Kippur. I am a Canopy of Peace. I know the secret of finding the essential harmony between the spiritual and the physical.

And, as we shall see, that is the message of Koheles. Come, let us learn.

<hr>

THE MEGILLAH

<hr>

תן חלק לשבעה ...
(קהלת 11:2)

Give
"Seven"
Its Due...
(Koheles 11:2)

REFLECTIONS ON MEGILLAS KOHELES

S HLOMO HAMELECH has given us two megillahs, or scrolls: *Shir HaShirim* and *Koheles*. *Shir HaShirim* teaches us how to love God; *Koheles,* how to fear Him. Love touches our hearts; fear, our minds.

Love does not deal with wisdom; its mode is intoxication: *He has taken me to the drinking chamber, has spread His love over me like a banner (Shir HaShirim* 2:4). The expression which Rambam favors when he discusses it is *shagah:* quite literally, to be out of one's mind. Love does not have its feet on the ground. The realities of everyday life touch it not at all.

Fear is a different story. Its mode is servitude, and therefore it requires a hard-nosed realism that must see things as they are. It faces life in the raw.

Nothing that is endemic to the human condition falls outside the ambit of its concerns: the ills of society and the individual; the frailties of both the leaders and the led; the farmer and the artisan; the righteous and the wicked, and, most poignantly, the fool. Koheles knows them all. They matter to him deeply. With all these in mind, he wages his battle against a life of meaningless vanity.

Our title is based upon Maharal (*Netzach*, Ch. 32), who teaches that in Torah thought the number seven symbolized the this-worldly while eight carries intimations of the Messianic Era.

At verse 11:2, Koheles exhorts us to "Give seven it's due …" Given what we have now learned, we may understand the phrase to mean that even the physical world has much to offer us in our service of God.

We shall learn that this idea is the central theme of our Megillah. That is why we have named this little collection of essays: *Give Seven Its Due.*

Finding Joy in Unlikely Places

KOHELES IS HARD! It's hard to translate, hard to understand and hard to penetrate to its core. It frustrates more than it illuminates and seems not to deliver what we expect from a megillah. We find no sharply focused message to engage our minds, no gripping narrative to move our hearts. There seems to be no tightly structured argument to ease our quest for understanding. We detect no logical progression from a clearly articulated question to an answer that leaves us informed and satisfied. We are thrown a patchwork of musings and jottings, cleanly etched pictures and shadowy presences, philosophy and elegy, homily and exhortation; and we are hard-put to make sense of it all.

Above all, *Koheles* has an image problem. If, as the megillah seems to assert again and again, all is vanity, something tells us that we would rather not know about it. Why frustrate ourselves by exposure to a message of such unrelieved negativism?

In this and the following essays, we propose to offer an analysis of the book's goal and attempt some careful definitions of the key phrases that give it body and nuance. We will discover that Koheles is concerned with teaching us how to function as servants of God amid the drabness and dross, the venality and pettiness, the struggles and defeats, and above all, the dreadful complexities and contradictions of a physical world from which God seems very far removed.

And wonder of wonders, we will learn that ours is a world of joy and fulfillment, affirmation and positivism. We will learn that there is nothing at all of *vanity* about it. *Vanity* is the defining characteristic of a life that is misdirected, lived under the sun, as we shall define that term.

When we do things right, our life breaks out of its shackles. Drabness turns to sparkle; the dross of the ordinary turns into the ringing triumph of a life well lived.

We will walk with Koheles, follow him in his search, think his thoughts, and arrive with him at his conclusions. In the end we will be able to sing with him his paean of praise to this, our own physical world: "Light is so sweet, it is so good for the eyes to behold the sun!" (11:7).

AVODAH MI'YIR'AH—TREMBLING BEFORE GOD

In our introductory passage, *Give "Seven" Its Due*, we contend that, in contrast to *Shir HaShirim* that talks of love, *Koheles* lays out for us the paths of serving God out of fear.

Let us examine this proposition and follow where it may lead. And let us note in passing that the megillah itself appears to confirm our thesis. When it ends with the words: "The sum of the matter when all has been considered: Fear God and keep His commandments for that is total man," that is not a fortuitous peculiarity but a calculated and necessary culmination to its central purpose. *Quod erat demonstrandum*, it says to us. We have demonstrated what we had set out to prove. There are problems in life, challenges and predicaments, to which only serving God out of fear can provide the correct response.

Given our discovery, we now have a criterion by which

we can attempt to understand the widely disparate issues with which Koheles grapples. We will be able to discover common ground among them as we recognize that they are clustered around this central theme. Each of them has characteristics that make valid grist for Koheles's mill. Each poses problems that are examined from the perspective of serving God out of fear, and each finds its solution within the compass of fear's reach.

We should now make an attempt to validate our thesis. Can we really affirm that the central theme of the megillah is to position a this-worldly orientation within the framework of serving God?

YIR'AH AND OLAM HAZEH: AWE AND THIS WORLD

We would do well to begin our analysis with the words of R. Eliyahu E. Dessler in *Michtav MeEliyahu* II p. 218:

> Fear [in contrast to love] defines divine service in its perfect form in the lower world [or, as we would put it, this world]. At this level of divine service man has to deal with the realities of physicality. He is called upon to make use of all it has to offer—but only for the sake of Heaven.

What does this mean?

It means that the lower world, the world in which physicality must be faced, is not hospitable to a love relationship with God. In such a relationship, the intellect may well become an impediment. We delight in our togetherness with the object of our adoration, and that closeness, by definition, precludes critical analysis that requires a stepping back, a viewing from the distance. In love there is no such thing. Love is the state in which we are lost in paradise.[1]

Not so serving God out of fear.

Service is the mode in which fear is expressed. Any servant would do well to examine carefully and understand well what is expected of him. When we meet God in love, we, as it were, lift ourselves beyond this-worldly considerations. When we stand submissively before Him as servants ready to do His bidding, we must open our minds to the countless problems which life in this endlessly beguiling, endlessly complex, endlessly threatening world, serves up to us.

If there is no wisdom, there can be no fear [of heaven] (*Pirkei Avos* 3:17). That says it all. And so, as we would expect, the search for wisdom is one of the great themes that animates Koheles. We can understand and sympathize with his restless experimentation, his determination to discover the correct way of making use of this world's bounties. True to his goal of clarifying the contours of serving God out of fear, he is determined to discover, by way of judicious use of wisdom, the rights and wrongs of this-worldly life.

IS OUR THESIS TENABLE?

We must, however, wonder whether we are not guilty of wishful thinking. Are we not attempting to impose a convenient theory upon an intractable reality? Does it make sense to have Koheles so vitally interested in a world that he has repeatedly described as vanity?

Yes, it makes a great deal of sense. For vanity is the description which Koheles (1:2–3) uses for a life lived *under the sun*.[2] Vanity is a state of moral stagnation, a condition in which we remain what we are, impervious to the invigorating challenge which our world becomes once we realize that it is amenable to sublimation.[3] Vanity is the state in which we are locked in a dungeon of enfeebling lethargy, morally stunted, frustrated and ultimately disillusioned, bitter and full of contempt and loathing for our smallness. All this is because we have not yet opened our hearts to the fear of God, because we live *under the sun*.

As we work our way through the megillah, we will find

that Koheles has something better to offer us. His is a message that parallels that of the *succah*. Sanctity can pervade the most mundane of your activities. You and your life can be good, very very good, if only you make your home in the shade.

Life

לולי תורתך שעשעי אז אבדתי בעניי (תהלים
קי"ט צ"ב)
*Were Your Torah not my constant delight I
would surely have perished in my affliction.
(Tehillim 119:92)*

Koheles and the Study of the Torah

T HERE is no getting around it: the word Torah does not
occur in *Koheles* even once.[1] What are we to make of
this? Is it possible that King Solomon would simply ignore
that which his father David had affirmed with the fervor expressed in the verse with which we headed our essay? Did
King Solomon himself not teach that the prayers of one who
refuses to listen to Torah are an abomination (*Mishlei* 28:9)?[2]
Could it be that this man, known as Yedidyah—God's beloved
(see *Shmuel* II 12:25)—did not love God's beloved Torah?[3]

Before we even begin our analysis, we should take notice
that Rashi to 8:15 cites a Midrash Aggadah that claims:

כל אכילה ושתיה שבקוהלת אינה אלא תלמוד תורה
*Every reference to "eating" and "drinking" in Koheles
is in reality a code word for the study of Torah.*

This is based on *Yeshayah* 55:1, where the words *Go, purchase and eat…* are assumed to be metaphorical and to refer to learning Torah. Apparently, then, eating and drinking is an appropriate metaphor for Torah study.[4]

But Rashi offers this as only an alternate explanation. In his first interpretation, he is perfectly willing to take *to eat and to drink* literally. Apparently, the Midrash here is not meant to supplant the literal meaning but only to augment it.

This leads us to a more general discussion of the relationship between *p'shat* and *derash*—simple meaning and homiletics—and more particularly how these two modes of interpretation color and contour the message of Koheles.

VARIOUS FORMS OF *P'SHAT* AND *DERASH*

For the purpose of our analysis we will concentrate on only three types of relationship between *p'shat* and *derash*, although there are certainly more. We will call them the Metaphor, the Divergence, and the Thickening.

1. THE METAPHOR: In the metaphor, we cannot speak of the *p'shat* sending a different message than does the *derash*. The *p'shat* is only the vehicle by which the message of the *derash* is to be conveyed.

We have an example of the Metaphor in *Shabbos* 63a. From *Tehillim* 45:4: "*Oh hero! Gird your sword to your thigh—it is your glory and your majesty,*" the Gemara attempts to prove that weapons are to be considered an ornament.[5] If they can be described as glory and majesty, they are clearly ornamental. The Gemara attempts to refute the proof: the verse is to be understood as a metaphor; the reference is not to a real warrior (whose weapons, far from being glory and majesty, are a disgrace) but to a Sage. It is an exhortation that he must keep his Torah knowledge (his glory and majesty) about him just as a warrior will never permit himself to be without his weapon.

In defense of the proof, the Gemara concedes the premise

that use of the military theme is to be understood as meta-phorical, but maintains that the suggested conclusion that weapons are an ornament is nevertheless valid. The literal meaning of the words must also be consistent with the truth. If an actual sword were not to be considered an ornament, it would be deficient as a metaphor for Torah knowledge.[6]

P'shat and *derash* are congruent here. There is only one message. *Tehillim* is not interested in glorifying a knight but in extolling the Sage with his vast store of Torah knowledge always ready to hand. If we understand *p'shat* as being identified with the thought that is being communicated, then there is no duality here at all.[7]

2. THE DIVERGENCE: We use this term to describe a case in which *p'shat* and *derash*, while entirely compatible with one another in the sense that they can both be true and even interrelated, diverge in their reading of the text.

An example of this would be *Bereishis* 25:28. There we learn, *Yitzchak loved Eisav, for game was in his mouth.* The first part of the phrase is plain enough: Yitzchak loved Eisav. But what does *for game was in his mouth* mean?

We quote Rashi: *In his mouth: as the Targum states, in the mouth of Yitzchak.* This appears to be Rashi's *p'shat* rendering. He bases it on the Aramaic Targum, which renders loosely: *because he ate from his game.* Hence: *... because [Eisav's] game was in [Yitzchak's] mouth.* Rashi then continues: *In the midrashic explanation the entire meaning of the word changes: for [Yitzchak] was game in [Eisav's] mouth. [Eisav] entrapped him and deceived him by [manipulating him with] his mouth.*

Now clearly the two interpretations are in no way contradictory and may even complement one another. It is possible that Yitzchak enjoyed eating Eisav's game[8] and that he also allowed himself to be manipulated by Eisav's cunning talk. The latter may even be an outgrowth of the former. Thus,

Yitzchak, who loved Eisav's game, was predisposed to believe him and therefore fell prey easily to his deceitful talk. But *p'shat* and *derash* do diverge when it comes to translation. According to the *p'shat, game* refers to the game which Eisav caught; according to the *derash*, it refers to Yitzchak. According to the *p'shat, his mouth* is Yitzchak's mouth; according to the *derash*, it is Eisav's.[9]

3. THE THICKENING: In this system the *derash* is simply a "thickening" or a deepened perception, an amplification of the *p'shat*. It is the *p'shat* at a more profound level.

An example of this thickening would be the midrashic assertion cited by Rashi at Koheles 8:15 that we quoted above: *The terms achilah and shesiyah when used in Koheles really refer to Torah study.*

Torah study can indeed be viewed as a kind of eating. What food does for the body, Torah accomplishes for the inner man. The *Tehillim* passage that we placed at the beginning of this essay, *Were Your Torah not my constant delight I would surely have perished in my affliction* (*Tehillim* 119:92), could, at a physical level, have been said about food. Without it we would perish in our affliction.

When, therefore, we have a verse like 2:24: *Is it not befitting that man should eat, drink...,* the correct meaning will be determined by the discerning sensitivity of the reader.[10] Where the one will see a steak, the other will see a *Teshuvas R' Akiva Eiger.*[11] Both interpretations are "correct." Neither of our two hypothetical readers really understands the other. The one will argue that learning is well and good, but that you cannot eat a book; the other will be quite certain that King Solomon would never have waxed lyrical over something as peripheral and uninteresting as eating. He knows very well from where his sustenance flows.[12]

Derash, here, thickens the *p'shat*. It penetrates to and

awakens latent resonances which a more superficial reading would have missed.

In such a *p'shat/derash* relationship, the *derash* obviously does not replace the *p'shat*. Both can lay claim to being the real message of the text. It will be the reader who decides which of the two describes the reality of his particular world.[13]

P'SHAT AND DERASH IN KOHELES

A careful reading of some of Rashi to *Koheles* yields that his perception of much of the *p'shat* and *derash* in this megillah is of the third variety. The *derash* is to be seen as a thickening or deepening of the *p'shat*, that, however, retains its own integrity. Often, the megillah communicates with us at two levels. We might almost say that there are two discrete worlds of which King Solomon speaks. There is the *p'shat* world of simple, worldly pleasures, simply and legitimately enjoyed provided that they are not subordinated to the baneful influence of *under the sun*. And then there is the *derash* world, more profoundly lived and experienced, where Torah and mitzvos are the only legitimate ideals.

We will go about our analysis by examining several verses that all seem to be saying much the same thing, and studying what Rashi says in explanation of each one of them. For easier examination we shall make a table so that each of the verses can be viewed together with the appropriate Rashi.

רש"י	קהלת	
...אחדל מן החכמה ואעסוק במשתה תמיד.	אמרתי אני בלבי לכה נא אנסכה בשמחה וראה בטוב [2:1] ...	1.
...שיאכל ושתה והראה את נפשו טוב, כלומר יתן לבו לעשות משפט וצדקה עם המאכל והמשתה ...	אין טוב באדם שיאכל ושתה והראה את נפשו טוב בעמלו גם זו ראיתי אני כי מיד האל־הים היא. [2:24]	2.
וראה טוב: תורה ומצוות.	וגם כל האדם שיאכל ושתה וראה טוב בכל עמלו מתת אל־הים היא. [3:13]	3.
מאשר ישמח במעשיו: ביגיע כפיו ישמח ויאכל ולא להרחיב כשאול נפשו לחמוד להתעשר להתרבות לא לו.	וראיתי כי אין טוב מאשר ישמח האדם במעשיו כי הוא חלקו ... [3:22]	4.
לאכול ולשתות, ולראות טובה: לעסוק בתורה שתהיא לקח טוב, ואל יקבץ הון רב אלא בחלק הניתן לו ישמח כי הוא חלקו.	הנה אשר ראיתי אני טוב אשר יפה לאכול ולשתות ולראות טובה בכל עמלו שיעמל תחת השמש ... כי הוא חלקו [5:17]	5.
שיהא שמח בחלקו ועוסק בפקודים ישרים משמחי לב ולא יהיה שטוף אחר הרבות הון ... כל מי שאינו שמח בחלקו ושטוף אחר הממון בא לידי עבירות גזל ואונאה ... ושאינו שמח בחלקו בענין אהבת אשתו שטוף אחרי הנשים להרהר אחר אשת איש. לאכול ולשמוח: ממה שנתן לו הקב"ה ולשמוח בחלקו. ומדרש אגדה, כל אכילה ושתיה שבקוהלת אינו אלא תלמוד תורה ...	ושבחתי אני את השמחה אשר אין טוב לאדם תחת השמש כי אם לאכל ולשתות ולשמוח [8:15] ...	6.

רש"י	קהלת
... אֱכֹל אֵיתָה הַצַדִיק שֶׁכְּבָר רָצָה הקב"ה מַעֲשֶׂיךָ הַטּוֹבִים וְתִזְכֶּה לְעוֹלָם הַבָּא, לֵךְ אֱכוֹל בְּשִׂמְחָה.	7. ... לֵךְ אֱכֹל בְּשִׂמְחָה לַחְמֶךָ [9:7]

	Koheles	Rashi
1.	*I said in my heart: Come now, I will try joy and see good. (2:1)*	I will not engage in wisdom but constantly involve myself in drinking.
2.	*Is it not good for a person to eat and drink and see good in his toil? This too, I saw, is from the hand of God. (2:24)*	That is to say, dedicate himself to being just and righteous with food and drink.
3.	*And also every person who eats and drinks and sees good in all his toil—that is a gift of God. (3:13)*	"And sees good" refers to Torah and mitzvos.
4.	*And I saw that there is nothing better than that a person should rejoice in his deeds, for that is his portion. (3:22)*	That a person should rejoice in his deeds: in the toil of his hands, and rejoice and eat and not broaden his soul like Sheol to desire wealth to acquire what is not his.
5.	*Behold I saw as good that is fine to eat and to drink and to see good in all one's toil that one engages in under the sun, for that is one's portion. (5:17)*	To eat and to drink and to see good: To engage in Torah, which is a "good gift," and not gather a massive fortune, but in the portion that He has given him, he should rejoice, for that is his portion.

	Koheles	Rashi
6.	*And I praised joy, for there is no good for a person under the sun except to eat and to drink and to rejoice.* (8:15)	He should rejoice in his portion and engage in righteous laws that rejoice the heart and not be driven to gain great wealth… Whoever is not joyful in his portion but is driven to attain money comes to the sins of thievery and dishonesty… and a person who is not joyful in his portion, in terms of loving his wife, is driven after women, to think about another man's wife. To eat and to drink: From that which the Holy One, blessed be He, gave him, and to rejoice in his portion. And a midrash aggadah states that the eating and drinking in Koheles refer only to Torah learning.
7.	*Go, eat your bread in joy.* (9:7)	But you, the righteous person whose good deeds, the Holy One, blessed be He, has already accepted, you will gain the world-to-come—so go, eat in joy.

For the purpose of our analysis, we will examine the three expressions which seem to be central to these selections: 1. seeing good; 2. eating and drinking; 3. joy.

1. SEEING GOOD: In #1, which is the first time in *Koheles* that the term occurs, Rashi is silent. Clearly it is to be taken literally and therefore does not require any definition. The context itself makes clear that at this stage of King Solomon's experimentation, there was to be no role for the pursuit of wisdom at all. He would allow joy to envelop him and live the good [physical] life.

In #2 Rashi renders "seeing the good" as "l'asos tzadaka u'mishpat," "being just and righteous" in #3 as "Torah and Mitzvos" and in #5 as "l'aosok b'Torah," "engaging in Torah."

It seems clear that the base meaning of the phrase is simply the good [physical] life, but, depending upon context, it can mean any number of things in the spiritual realm. The *derash* calls upon us to thicken the meaning of the *p'shat*.

2. TO EAT AND TO DRINK: In numbers 2, 4, 5, 6 (in the first interpretation), and 7, Rashi takes the term to mean literally to eat and to drink. In most of these instances, he suggests that Koheles is exhorting us to be happy with what we have and to leave grandiose ambitions aside. It is only in #6 that he notes that according to the Midrash Aggadah all mention of eating and drinking, certainly including all those references in the passages which he had previously interpreted literally, should really be read as having Torah study in mind. Clearly the *derash* calls upon us to read beneath the surface, and to perceive that man does not live by bread alone. There are those among us who are sustained more by the Torah that they learn than by the food that they eat.

3. JOY: In #1 Rashi is silent, but the entire context makes it abundantly clear that physical enjoyment is meant. In #4 Rashi clearly takes it in physical terms, but in #6 he suggests that joy might be found in immersing oneself in righteous laws, because such involvement gladdens the heart. Once more we can draw the conclusion that Rashi recognizes that joy can be experienced in many different forms. One can be happy with the modest lot which God has assigned to him (#3) or, at a more profound level, with the *righteous laws* as in #6.

TORAH AND WISDOM

We wish to propose that what is true for the three concepts

that we examined above is also true for the idea of wisdom as it is used in Koheles. There are many instances in which Rashi insists that the term refers to Torah,[14] but there are also cases where he does not. This seems to have occurred where the context simply does not lend itself naturally to such an interpretation.

Thus, for example, at 2:17–22, Koheles examines the plight of one who has expended enormous thought and energy in building up something that is worthwhile, and is worried that his heirs might misuse or even squander all that he has so lovingly wrought. This fear is expressed in verse 19 as follows:

ומי יודע החכם יהיה או סכל וישלוט בכל עמלי שעמלתי
ושחכמתי ...

And who knows if he will be wise or foolish? And he will rule over all my toil, from when I toiled and gained wisdom...

And again in verse 21:

... כי יש אדם שעמלו בחכמה

For there is a person who toils with wisdom...

Certainly it is not the study of Torah which is meant here.

It is not what is meant again at 7:11, where Koheles sets forth the advantages of combining wisdom with wealth. The text makes it clear that this combination would be beneficial to *those who see the sun*. Now Rashi, based on *Nedarim* 30b, defines this expression as referring to all humans, including non-Jews. This makes it impossible to identify wisdom in this context with Torah.

Accordingly, we are led to the conclusion that the term wisdom is to be understood precisely as we have the other three expressions discussed above.[15] There is *p'shat* and there is *derash*. At the *p'shat* level, the meaning is that which strikes one at the first uncritical glance—and in our case that would be wisdom taken in its broadest sense. But then there is the thickening *derash*, which draws our attention to other, more profound possibilities. It is at that level that wisdom is identical with Torah.

THE MESSAGE

Is it possible to talk of a main and a subsidiary message in the context of *p'shat* and *derash*? Can it be said concerning either of them that the message which it conveys is more in keeping with the true intention of the writer than is the other?

We suggest that there may be differences between the various forms of *derash* which we have delineated above. It seems likely that in the category which we named Divergence, the two messages are of equal import, while in the Thickening category there may well be a qualitative difference between the various levels.

Thus, in the matter of Yitzchak's love for Eisav, there are two apparently equally compelling explanations. Yitzchak enjoyed the game which Eisav, the consummate hunter, brought home, and he also fell prey to that same hunter's cunning wiles. There seems no persuasive reason to prefer the one explanation over the other.

That is not the case when we talk about the *derash* thickening the *p'shat*. We can certainly imagine King Solomon hoping that people will not satisfy themselves with a surface reading, but find the drive and energy to discover the world beneath.

Koheles then may be said to be communicating at two levels. The *cognoscenti* will recognize the message beneath the message and learn that only Torah can energize a truly significant life. Those with whom this idea does not resonate will be guided to fulfillment at a more superficial level.

It is to those to whom the *p'shat* of *Koheles* is directed that we devote the following essay.

וְלַשִּׂמְחָה מַה זּוֹ עֹשָׂה

...And as for joy, of what use could it possibly be? (2:2)

וְשִׁבַּחְתִּי אֲנִי אֶת הַשִּׂמְחָה ...

Then I realized the advantages of joy... (5:18)

... The one refers to joy taken in a mitzvah, the other to joy that is taken in something that is not a mitzvah. (Shabbos 30b)

Living Life to the Fullest

Joy in the simple things of life looms large on the agenda which Koheles lays down for us.

Let us take a sampling:

1. אֵין טוֹב בָּאָדָם שֶׁיֹּאכַל וְשָׁתָה וְהֶרְאָה אֶת נַפְשׁוֹ טוֹב בַּעֲמָלוֹ גַּם זֶה רָאִיתִי אָנִי כִּי מִיַּד הָאֱלֹהִים הִיא. (ב כד)

   Is it not befitting that man should eat, drink and permit himself to appreciate life as a result of the labors that he performs? This is one of those things that I, for myself, perceive as a gift from God's hand... (2:24)

2. יָדַעְתִּי כִּי אֵין טוֹב בָּם כִּי אִם לִשְׂמוֹחַ וְלַעֲשׂוֹת טוֹב בְּחַיָּיו. וְגַם כָּל הָאָדָם שֶׁיֹּאכַל וְשָׁתָה וְרָאָה טוֹב בְּכָל עֲמָלוֹ מַתַּת אֱלֹהִים הִיא. (ג יב יג)

   I realized that in all these circumstances, the only real good is to rejoice, and throughout his life, to do that

*which is good. Moreover, that "total man" should eat,
drink and appreciate life as a result of his labors—that
is a gift from God. (3:12–13)*

3. וראיתי כי אין טוב מאשר ישמח האדם במעשיו כי הוא
חלקו... (ג כב)

*Then I perceived that there is nothing better than that
man should rejoice in his accomplishments—for that
is his portion (3:22)[16]*

4. גם כל האדם אשר נתן לו האלהים עשר ונכסים והשליטו
לאכל ממנו ולשאת את חלקו ולשמוח בעמלו זה מתת
אלהים היא. (ה יח)

*Moreover, "total man," to whom God granted wealth
and possessions, and also empowered him to take advantage of it and make use of his portion, rejoicing in
his labors—[All] this is a gift from God (5:18)*

5. ושבחתי אני את השמחה אשר אין טוב לאדם תחת
השמש כי אם לאכל ולשתות ולשמוח והוא ילונו בעמלו
ימי חייו אשר נתן לו האלהים תחת השמש. (ח טו)

*Then I realized the advantages of joy, in as much as
there is no real good for man under the sun other than
to eat, drink and be happy. For only this will accom-
pany him during his labors throughout the life which
God has granted him beneath the sun. (8:15)[17]*

6. לך אכל בשמחה לחמך ושתה בלב טוב יינך כי כבר רצה
האלהים את מעשיך. (ט ז)

*Go, eat your bread with joy, and with a happy heart
drink your wine ... (9:7)*

Koheles never ceases to surprise us. In a megillah focused
so insistently on themes that give us precious little to be
happy about, he repeatedly counsels quiet satisfaction with
life's simple pleasures. We are to eat, drink and enjoy the in-
significant banalities of life—and feel good about it.[18]

Something seems out of harmony. It is not only the apparently blatant contradiction between the two thoughts heading this chapter that cries for solution. Rather, it seems incongruous that our megillah should be so affirmative about physical pleasures[19] when the ubiquity of vanity colors so many of its passages.

FALSE ASSUMPTIONS

Solutions to seemingly intractable problems often lie in a re-examination of cherished assumptions. We need to do some critical questioning about some of the ideas concerning *Koheles* that we tend to take for granted.

Let us then test the following proposition: *Koheles* is a megillah that condemns this-worldly activity as irredeemably futile. What profit does man have for all his labor that he toils beneath the sun? (1:3) Is this true or not so true?

To get a clear picture, we should first dispose of the apparent contradiction with which we began.

Koheles's rejection of joy as a useful mode must be read in context. It appears in Chapter 2 as an expression of King Solomon's disappointment with one of a series of experiments that he had launched in order to discover the contours of a life ideally lived. After having rejected various models in which the quest for wisdom was central, he had thought that perhaps it would make sense to devote all his energies to a pursuit of joy:

... לכה נא אנסכה בשמחה וראה בטוב

I said in my heart: Come now, I will try joy and see good. (2:1)

At that stage of his investigations it seemed to make sense. Everything else which he had tried had failed. Perhaps pure physicality could do what a futile and frustrating search for wisdom could not. Perhaps it could be an avenue to an appreciation of God's bounty. Why not try?

It soon became apparent that it would not work. *What does joy accomplish?* Joy at the center could simply not support life's burdens. It could not satisfy.

That is all. The phrase says no more than that. We are left with the tantalizing possibility that, on a larger canvas, the ability to appreciate life's simpler gifts might quite possibly add some very special beauty. Let us examine this proposition.

SOME MORE DEFINITIONS

The passages that we quoted above contain at least two expressions that bear closer analysis: *toil* (1, 2, 4 and 5) and *the whole man*, or *total man* (2 and 4).

First let us examine *toil*:

Our instinctive reaction to the word is one of unrelieved negativism. It comes to us from 1:3, the verse with which Koheles begins his reflections and which can therefore be counted on to make a lasting impression:

מה יתרון לאדם בכל עמלו שיעמל תחת השמש
What benefit does man have from all his labor if he invests his energies beneath the sun?

There it is, weighted down with all the pathos of the seven vanities of 1:2:

20. הבל הבלים אמר קוהלת הבל הבלים הכל הבל.
Vanity of vanities, said Koheles. Vanity of vanities, everything is vanity.

What uselessness! What utter futility!

Toil seems beyond redemption. There is just no point to it at all.

So why the positive note in our passages? What has happened to make toil respectable?

Shabbos 30b supplies the answer. The opprobrium of the earlier verse is limited to toil that takes place *under the sun.* If the toil can be described as *before the sun,* as being motivated by the Torah that preceded the sun, then one may find great profit in it.

We note that none of the examples that we cited at the beginning of our discussion, with the exception of #5, has the toil of which it talks take place *under the sun.* (And concerning this one example, see Endnote #2, above.)

Thus, it is simply untrue to say that Koheles has nothing good to say about the mundane activities that occupy so much of our lives. They can obviously be abused. But they can also provide, as we shall shortly see, a most benign context for a life lived in the service of God.[21]

Before we begin to examine this proposition, we will look at the second term that we noted above. What precisely is the meaning of *total man* as opposed to simply *man* or *the man*?

The obvious source for clarification of this issue is the penultimate verse in the megillah:

סוף דבר הכל נשמע את האל־הים ירא ואת מצותיו שמור
כי זה כל האדם.

The sum of the matter when all has been considered: Fear God and keep His commandments for that is total man.

What is the sense of *total man*?

We turn to Maharal (*Nesivos Olam, Nesiv HaAhavah* 1). He avers that God-fearing man is called *the man*, with the definite article, because he is that special person whom God had in mind when He created the world. Hence the expression *total man*, literally, *all of the man.*

How so? Because the numerical equivalent of *ha'adam—the man*—is fifty, the same as that of *kol—all*—that expresses the idea of totality. *Kol ha'adam* is man in his ideal state. By contrast, *adam—man*—without the definite article, the un-special, ordinary man, has the numerical equivalent of forty-five, equaling that of *mah—what*—which connotes nothing-ness or emptiness.[22]

In the spirit of Maharal's idea, we have translated *kol ha'adam* as *total man*.

GETTING THINGS TOGETHER

We are now ready to examine our sources and to come to grips with what, in light of our analysis of the terms used, these might reveal.

They, or at least numbers 2 and 4, are telling us that as surely as man can only be said to be complete if he fears God and keeps His commandments (12:13), so too, if he wishes to be really whole, he must have his two feet firmly planted in life as it is lived in this world; he must eat, drink, work honestly for a living and be a good neighbor, a productive member of society. That is God's will and that is how His true servant will serve Him.

Fair enough. But why did God choose just this particular battleground as the arena in which we are to win our victories? Why does God insist that we get our hands dirty in his service?[23]

In order to gain perspective we should momentarily step outside the book and turn to the Gemara for some insights concerning the source and inspiration of the religious life.

LOVING THE "OTHER"

Clearly, based on what we have just learned, Koheles seems to feel that religious perfection must not only find itself in harmony with well-balanced mundane existence, but cannot be fully realized without it. That is a stunning revelation. However, it is familiar to us from another context. Between this and the definition of Judaism that, centuries later, Hillel HaZaken immortalized, there appears to be an uncanny similarity.

The story is well-known. A non-Jew approached Hillel expressing an interest in becoming Jewish provided that he could be taught the whole Torah while he was standing on one foot. Hillel accepted the challenge. The essence of Torah can be wrapped up in the words: "What is hateful to you, do not do to another. All else is commentary."

This audacious assertion that Judaism, in its essence, can be reduced to a negative formulation of the Torah's demand that we love our neighbors as we do ourselves, makes no ripple at all upon the smooth surface of our theological certitudes. We have been taught to read this passage as a vindication of Hillel's patience and understanding as opposed to the apparently unforgiving and unbending demands for uncompromised truth that was the hallmark of Shammai's bearing. In the process, our critical faculties have been lulled into passivity. We tend to miss the realization that Hillel's claim is absolutely revolutionary. By what right does he take one of the Torah's mitzvos, one that appears without fanfare or any other form of particularization among the many other mitzvos in *Kedoshim*, and claim centrality for it to the extent that all else is commentary?

Moreover, why does Hillel go out of his way to drain this most astounding mitzvah of its color and excitement? Why the pallid negative instead of the pulsating positive? Why pretend that we are bidden only to refrain from hurting when, in reality, God trusted us so much more, trusted our ability to love?

Where the Torah challenges us, Hillel appears to be satisfied with an appeal to self-interest. His suggestion that we consult our own feelings in order to ascertain appropriate behavior patterns, smacks of the famous assertion of *The Kuzari* (2:48) that even among a band of robbers some form of common decency must prevail. The Torah is more altruistic than that. It does not suggest that we love so that we might be loved. Where the Torah summons us to greatness, Hillel seems to recommend only prudence.

Is this really all that lies at the essence of Judaism? Is the Jew no more than one who subscribes to the tenets of civilized behavior? If this is all we have to say to the world, were the blood and horror of our dreadful history really worthwhile?

Above all, and here we return to our thoughts concerning Koheles, is Hillel not postulating a secular rather than a religious core to Judaism? Is not the moral obligation to treat others as we ourselves would wish to be treated the credo of the secular humanist?[24] How then can this principle be said to encapsulate the teachings of Judaism?

Where does God figure in Hillel's answer? Can there be a formulation of Judaism's basic teaching that does not even mention Him? Rashi has a remarkable suggestion. The Torah speaks of loving our friend as we do ourselves. Well, Rashi points out, God too is our Friend (based on *Mishlei* 27:10). He too has the right to demand that we treat Him with consideration. Would we not wish that our commands not be ignored? We must be careful, then, not to ignore His.

The implications are shattering. We cannot care for God unless we have first learned to care for man. Humanism bids us, once the truth of God's existence is stipulated, to live as men of religion.

The theory is simple enough. Man is either self-centered or other-centered. If he knows only his own needs, cares not at all for the sensitivities of another, then even God can be no more than peripheral to his concerns.

We asked how Hillel has the right to turn one mitzvah out of many into the irreducible core of Judaism and why he would seemingly devalue it by turning the positive command into an ultimately self-serving and uninspiring negative. The answer to both questions may be that Hillel did not have the mitzvah in mind at all. He was simply enunciating a psychological truth that, by its very nature, requires no scriptural mandate. It is an absolute given, rooted in human nature that, much as R. Chaim Vital claims concerning the ethical moment, must be assumed before the Torah is ever given. The Torah, to use Hillel's words, is no more than the commentary to this elemental quality; in the sense that its purpose is to refine and develop all that is good and worthy in the human potential.

We recognize a similar thought process in *Koheles*. Only those who have learned to live well with the world and all that it has to offer, can aspire to live well with God. Only those who have developed their full human potential will ultimately realize that the entirety of their humanity is fear of God and conscientious adherence to His commands.

Our purpose must always be to serve God in our role as *total man*. That is the meaning of living life to the fullest.

Question Marks

Problems

IN THE REAL WORLD, there are a great many things that are not as we would wish them to be. Koheles, as part of his quest for clarity, touches on many of them. Occasionally, he suggests a solution. Sometimes he merely bemoans what he perceives as the inescapable given of a life lived "under the sun."

There is no doubt that the most troublesome of the issues that he must face is that of theodicy. He struggles to understand a just God who, to all appearances, often seems to act unjustly. It is simply a fact that, too often, the wicked thrive obscenely and the righteous undergo the most dreadful of sorrows.

These are facts. They present a problem. Koheles must deal with it.

How does he go about it? Let us take one example from Chapter 8:

י.   ‏... גם זה הבל.

10. *... Also the following is vanity.*

יא.   אשר אין נעשה פתגם מעשה הרעה מהרה על כן מלא לב בני האדם בהם לעשות רע.

11. *Because the sentence for wrongdoing is not executed quickly, men are encouraged to do evil.*

יב. אשר חטא עשה רע מאת ומאריך לו כי גם יודע אני אשר
יהיה טוב ליראי האל־הים אשר ייראו מלפניו.

12. *That a sinner does what is wrong for a hundred ... and
He is patient with him. Yet nevertheless I am aware
that it will be well with those who fear God, those that
show fear before Him.*

יג. וטוב לא יהיה לרשע ולא יאריך ימים כצל אשר איננו ירא
מלפני אל־הים.

13. *But that it will not be well with the wicked and he will
not long endure—like a shadow—because he does not
fear God (8:10–13).*

Koheles is clearly attempting to grapple with the problem.
He poses some pointed questions, but in the second part of
verse 12 he assures us that in the end things will turn out as
they should.

We are left with a vague feeling of dissatisfaction. Not only
because justice delayed is justice denied, but because Koheles offers no basis at all for his optimism. He is "aware that
all will be well..." but that is all.

Whence this optimism? Certainly, nothing but a thor-
ough analysis of these difficult verses will get us where we
need to go.

The chart on the opposite page makes it clear that verses
11 and 12 are styled as *a b a b*, meaning that the first part of
verse 12 parallels the first part of verse 11, and that the same
is true of the second halves.

The *a* sections of both verses seem to face the identical di-
lemma. Our instincts tell us that retribution for evil should
come fast and furious on the heels of the transgression; and
our eyes tell us that this simply does not happen.

After that, the two verses part ways. Verse 11 bemoans the
fact that as a result of this seemingly wanton delay, people
are propelled into a pattern of wickedness, while verse 12 affirms unimpaired trust in God's perfect justice.

44

11. *a* אשר אין נעשה פתגם מעשה הרעה מהרה ...

That since the sentence for wrongdoing is not executed quickly...

b על כן מלא לב בני האדם בהם לעשות רע.

Men are encouraged to do evil

12. *a* אשר חטא עשה רע מאת ומאריך לו ...

That a sinner does what is wrong for a hundred … and He is patient with him.

b כי גם יודע אני אשר יהיה טוב ליראי האל־הים אשר יראו מלפניו.

Yet nevertheless I am aware that it will be well with those who fear God, those that show fear before Him.

13. וטוב לא יהיה לרשע ולא יאריך ימים כצל אשר איננו ירא מלפני אל־הים.

But that it will not be well with the wicked and he will not long endure—like a shadow—because he does not fear God.

How do we explain the difference? It would seem to have its provenance in the divergent views of *men* (11b) on the one hand and *I* (12b) on the other. *Men,* the men in the street, will allow themselves to be swept away[1] by their surface impressions and, in the face of perceived injustice, opt for a life of depravity. Koheles himself—*I*—can avoid this pitfall.

Given this insight, the way is open to further analysis. Let us begin with the puzzling *me'as* of verse 12. The word is the construct form of *me'ah,* a hundred. But the connection is missing. A hundred what? Rashi notes the problem and concludes that we have here a truncated phrase that could theoretically end with any unit—a hundred days, a hundred years, a hundred thousands and so on.

Well and good. But why the truncation? What is the point of leaving a blank? It would seem that this is a literary artifice designed to give the reader leeway to extend the time-frame to infinity. If any unit had been mentioned, it would by definition have limited the concept to a specific and specified duration. One hundred years is, at the end of the day, only one hundred years. By having to deal with a simple, unmodified *hundred of…*, the reader is, as it were, invited to fill in whatever he wants. Nothing is too long; anything is possible.

This reading yields another major difference between the two verses.

11. ‏... אשר אין נעשה ... מהרה
That is not executed quickly

12. ‏אשר ... עושה ... מאת ומאריך לו ...
That a sinner does what is wrong for a hundred … and
He is patient with him.

Verse 11 deals with a much shorter period than does verse 12. In verse 11 the punishment does not come as fast as we would wish. In verse 12 it seems never to come at all.

There is another difference between the two verses that seems worthy of note.

11. ‏אשר אין נעשה פתגם מעשה הרעה ...
That since the sentence for wrongdoing is not executed
quickly…

12. ‏אשר חטא עשה רע ...
That a sinner does what is wrong…

Thus verse 11 talks of the sin, while verse 12 talks of the sinner. Verse 11 worries about an abstract question of justice delayed, while verse 12 has to watch a flesh and blood sinner living a life of security and happiness with never a care in the world.

We conclude that Koheles himself, in verse 12, faces a much harder test than do the people in verse 11. They deal with a theory which does not work quite the way it should; while he has to watch the actual sinner live the good life with no end at all in sight.

And a strange thing happens. While they immediately lose their bearings, he not only maintains his religious integrity, but finds the source of his strength in the very problem that he has to face.

Herewith we have Koheles's description of his own experience:

PROBLEM

אשר חטא עשה רע מאת ומאריך לו ...

That a sinner does what is wrong for a hundred ... and He is patient with him.

SOLUTION

a כי גם יודע אני אשר יהיה טוב ליראי האל־הים אשר ייראו מלפניו.

Yet nevertheless I am aware that it will be well with those who fear God, those that show fear before Him.

b וטוב לא יהיה לרשע ולא יאריך ימים כצל אשר איננו ירא מלפני אל־הים.

But that it will not be well with the wicked and he will not long endure—like a shadow—because he does not fear God.

These verses present a number of major difficulties:

1.   The *a* section of the solution deals with the delayed reward of the righteous. This problem has not been raised. Why mention it?

2.   If for some reason it should be taken up, why does it precede the *b* section which is the direct answer to the problem which was raised?

3.   The assertion of the *b* section stands in blatant contradiction to what was stated in the problem. The problem asserted that the evil-doer was being given an infinite [*hun-*

dred of …] grace period without having to suffer the consequences of his actions, while *b* avers that this infinity is in fact as insubstantial as a shadow. Which is true?

The answer to the first and second points probably lies in the use of *also* in the phrase *yet nevertheless* (literally, *also*) *I am aware*. The implication is that *it will be well with those who fear God, those that show fear before Him* relates to *that a sinner does what is wrong for a hundred … and He is patient with him …* as a conclusion relates to the premise from which it is yielded.

Just as this is so, so too is this. The logic is as follows: The very fact that the wicked occasionally enjoy long and prosperous lives in spite of their wickedness, shows that not everything has to happen immediately. For the moment, we may leave aside the rationale for these unexpected time lapses. It is, however, a fact. This itself, helps me to deal with the sometimes unconscionable time which the righteous must wait until they receive their just reward. I understand that if punishment may take a while in coming, so too might reward.

Hence the word *also*.[2]

It transpires that the *a* part of the SOLUTION section is less an answer to, than a mirror image of the problem that has been posed. It is true that the plight of the righteous had not been formally enunciated in the statement of the problem. But there is no doubt at all that it is, indeed must be, lurking in the background.

It enjoys pride of place in the SOLUTION section because while an answer (*b*) stands outside the question, a virtual paraphrase (*a*) is the question itself in a different guise.

A paraphrase ought to precede an answer. In the SOLUTION section *a* rightly precedes *b*.

What of our third question? Is the insubstantial shadow not the very opposite of the unmodified and therefore the unlimited *hundred of…*?

Of course it is, and that is the whole point.

Again and again, Koheles comes to the conclusion that God's ways are inscrutable. See 7:14, quoted in Endnote #1, or at 8:17: *…Indeed, man cannot fathom the events that occur under the sun, inasmuch as man tries strenuously to search, but cannot fathom them. And even though a wise man would presume to know, he cannot fathom them.*

What then remains for wisdom to do? It can help us fashion an attitude. It can help us cope. Time lapses, at least as they are experienced by us, are not absolute. The same period can seem like an eternity to one person and like a flash of lightning to another.

In verse 2 of chapter 8, Koheles describes himself. The most accurate translation of his self-definition would probably be: *As for me, [my very nature is defined as one who is constantly confronted by the words], Be alert to the words of the King!*[3]

That same *I* is in play in our section.

For such a one, the longest time lapse can seem like only a passing shadow.

There really is no enigma at all.

Not every difficulty has a solution which we can grasp. Not every problem will yield to even the most rigorous analysis. Sometimes we simply will not know the answer. However, if we cannot control the world, we can at least control our attitudes. And that makes all the difference.

Making Do

IN THE PREVIOUS CHAPTER, Koheles taught that although some problems are simply intractable, attitude can make a difference. We do not need to allow our frustrations to drive us into bitter rejection of all that we hold holy. Instead, we can use our heads and literally change our minds. Big questions can become little questions, and with little ones we can deal.

Let us follow Koheles as he works his way through some of the other conundrums with which any thinking person must come to grips.

> יש הבל אשר נעשה על הארץ אשר יש צדיקים אשר מגיע אלהם כמעשה הרשעים ויש רשעים שמגיע אלהם כמעשה הצדיקים אמרתי שגם זה הבל.
>
> *There is a form of vanity upon the earth. The righteous are sometimes treated as though they had acted wickedly, while the wicked are sometimes treated as though they had acted righteously. I declared, "This too is vanity" (8:14).*

While Koheles's problem is clear enough, the wording he uses begs for analysis. The first phrases reads: *There is a form of vanity upon the earth.* Taken by itself, it is not particularly striking; but in the context of the megillah as a whole, it stands out. This is so because while *under the sun* and *under the sky* are used all the time,[4] our verse is the very first one in which *upon the earth* replaces one of these other two expressions. Is there a reason for this? There appears to be no special need for a new expression, since we return effortlessly to *under the sun* in the very next verse. Why then the new wording?

If we are to get an accurate sense of the expression, we must derive it from the context. First, then, we will make a small digression and try to understand a little better the problem which Koheles poses. Translated literally, the above verse (8:14) reads, *The righteous are sometimes treated as though there touches them something like the deed of the wicked, while the wicked are sometimes treated as though there touches them something like the deed of the righteous.*

We analyze as follows:

The use of the word *to touch* in the causative occurs both when the touching is intentional—as for example in *Yeshaya* 5:8: *Woe to those who cause one house to touch another*; and when it is not, as in *Shir HaShirim* 2:12: *the season of song is touching upon us.*

Which is meant here? Does Koheles suggest that the righteous are intentionally made to suffer and the wicked to thrive, or does he suggest that it just happens like that without anyone intending that justice should be thus offended?

The latter meaning is of course correct. Certainly Koheles would not wish to claim that God acts capriciously, rewarding the wicked and making the righteous suffer. So we are left with assuming that things just happen as they do. How are we to understand this?

This is where *upon the earth* is of help. This expression, in contrast to the other two, is entirely value free. *Under the sun* and *under the sky* have an agenda. In *Living Life to the Fullest*, we have seen that *under the sun* is weighted by the futility of this-worldly endeavors. In the Endnote earlier in this chapter, we have seen that *under the sky* intimates the awe that is born of a distance that can never be bridged. *Upon the earth* is free of all such freight. It describes life as it is lived. It recognizes that ours is a physical world, and that in a physical world there are limitations to the extent to which God is willing to interfere in the orderly progression of physical realities.

Let us work out the implications. The second paragraph of the *Shema* tells us that adherence to, and punctilious observance of, God's commands will be rewarded by ample rainfall. Drought is to be the wage of sin.

Now let us imagine a righteous farmer surrounded by wicked neighbors. These people are to be punished by the withholding of rain from their fields. There is no reason why he should suffer with them. Nevertheless, in the real world God will not send rain upon his little field and leave the rest of the valley arid. This righteous man will have to garner his reward in a different currency. The reverse, of course, is also true. A wicked farmer who has chosen his neighbors wisely will not be denied the rain which anyway has to fall all around him. God is sufficiently all-powerful to make sure that he will receive his punishment by some other means (R' Elchanan Wasserman, *Kovetz Ma'amarim*).

In the first case, the righteous farmer is treated as badly as his wicked neighbors. In the second, the wicked farmer enjoys the same benefits as do the righteous men among whom he lives.

That is the *vanity* which Koheles perceived. Its mode is *upon the earth*. It is an inescapable function of God's determination that our world be governed by nature. God's miraculous intervention will occur only under the most unusual circumstances. This is just the way things are.

So what does Koheles do? His immediate reaction (verse 15) is to give up the quest for understanding. Instead of losing sleep at night (verse 16), he will concentrate on living positively. He will learn to love the simple pleasures, and sing the paean to joy which we have analyzed in *Living Life to the Fullest*. He is willing to leave it at that.

But not for long. The inelegance with which life seems to dispense its favors keeps nagging away at him and leaves him no peace. There is no "one size fits all" solution. And so, Koheles examines the problem from another perspective. Let us follow him:

זה רע בכל אשר נעשה תחת השמש כי מקרה אחד לכל וגם לב בני האדם מלא רע והוללות בלבבם בחייהם ואחריו אל המתים.

This is an evil about all things that go on under the sun: that the same fate awaits us all.

Therefore the heart of man is full of evil; and madness is in their heart during their life, and after that they go to the dead.

כי מי אשר יבחר [יחבר] אל כל החיים יש בטחון כי לכלב חי הוא טוב מן האריה המת.

For he who is attached to all of life has hope, a live dog being better than a dead lion. (9:3–4)

What is being said here? A careful analysis of the language would serve us well. We have a grammatical irregularity which can point us in the right direction, and which may well be the key to a true understanding of the passage. The text of the second half of the first verse reads as follows:

... והוללות בלבבם בחייהם ואחריו אל המתים

...and madness is in their heart during their lives, and after that they go to the dead.

Before we go to the grammatical irregularity, a little background is in order. The exact flavor of the word that we have translated as *madness* would be that of a madness born of confusion, of conflicting impressions, a perplexity born of contradictions and incongruencies. This is logical enough in context.

Now this *madness* is said to be the condition of *their lives.* What is added by this description?

We are now ready for the grammatical irregularity of which we spoke earlier. It is clear that the phrase "… and after that they go to the dead" refers to "their lives." After this life that has been spent in the confused madness of their frustrations, they have nowhere to go but to the grave.

This is all well and good. But *lives* is in the plural, whereas *after it* is in the singular. *After it* is irregular and illogical.

Why this strange usage? Why the singular pronoun for the plural noun? We will understand this better once we have come to grips with another unusual expression in the next verse.

For he who is attached to all of life. What exactly is the difference between *life* and *all of life*?[5]

Life is multi-faceted. It constantly dangles myriads of sparkling options before us, daring us to be brave, to be innovative, to be true to the particular mix of talents, traits and predilections which make up our unique personality.

Life is a plural noun. It cannot and must not be otherwise.

But the very richness of the offering, the sheer abundance of life's possibilities, makes a unifying and ordering discipline a must. In the absence of such control lies madness.

And madness leaves no discretion. The multiplicity of choices ends up in one-dimensional, drab and draining confusion. That is the *madness* of which our passage speaks. And that is why the tragedy of that *madness* is expressed in that it is *during their lives*, and why afterwards the singular *after it*, so striking in its irregularity, is used. Koheles is pointing out the sorrow and the pity of converting a life, which could yield such a profusion of choices (*life, pl.*) into monochromatic (*after it, sing.*) listlessness. Only someone who is attached to *all* the living, the whole of life, to whom all options are open, can have the hope of turning his frustrations to advantage.[6]

This, then, is the advice which Koheles has to give those of us who are plagued by the many questions which seem to have no answer at all. Do not permit your frustrations to sow confusion and deflect you from the exhilarating profusion of challenges and choices which life, bravely and intelligently lived, offers you.

Learn to live with question marks. There is much living to be done, many choices to be made, many challenges to be met in a busy, positive, constructive and creative life. You will continue to have doubts, but these can be relegated to the periphery; they can be placed in reasonable perspective. They too present a challenge. But it is only one among many. You will either find the solution or not. It doesn't really matter. Life is its own reward.

Prisms

How do we shape up as human beings? Is God happy with what He has wrought? Koheles has his doubts.

לבד ראה זה מצאתי, אשר עשה האל־הים את האדם ישר והמה בקשו חשבונות רבים.

Note carefully that I discovered the following: God created man with an inclination towards a straightfor-ward grasp of reality, but, instead, they insisted on all kinds of complications. (7:29)[7]

What exactly had God intended? Certainly He did not wish us to walk through life like so many "Pollyanas," pretending that all is wonderful when that is clearly not the truth. Life is just not lived that way. Only a fool has no problems. What is so wrong with an awareness of life's complexities? Is that not just another way of being a hard-headed pragmatist?

Let us turn to the next verse and see whether an analysis of its teachings can set us on the right path:

מי כהחכם

Great are the wise!

ומי יודע פשר דבר

Who else besides them can get to the essence of things, thus finding a path between seemingly conflicting needs.

חכמת אדם תאיר פניו

Man's wisdom lights up his face.

ועז פניו ישנא (8:1)

He stands out because of the sense of power that emanates from his face.[8]

Here apparently is the solution. The problem had been that men allowed themselves to be distracted by many different kinds of complications from the path that God had set for them. There must be a way, other than one of airy optimism, of dealing with the many, often reasonable, considerations which intrude upon us, without compromising the integrity with which God has endowed us.

As Koheles ponders this conundrum, the solution hits him. It is really all so simple. Only the truly wise will know how to truly live. The secret is in their minds. Why?

Because they know *peisher davar—the essence of things.* We have translated, or better, paraphrased this concept above. Our rendering is more elaborate than the simple wording in the Hebrew. The time has come to explain.

Rashi offers two possible translations for *peisher.* It could mean interpretation (equivalent to the word *pisron*), or it could mean compromise (*pesharah*).[9] The very ambiguity of the word leads us to surmise that the two concepts are related. To reach an equitable compromise between conflicting demands, it is necessary to interpret. We must strip away the disposable husk from the non-negotiable core in order that the fundamental commonality of interest can be revealed.

We adopt our paraphrase accordingly: *peisher davar* is the comprehension of the essence of things (*pisron*), such that a path can be found between outwardly colliding needs (*pesharah*). That, only the wise man can do.[10]

What, then, is that *essence of things*? What is the unifying theme which can quiet the ugly clamor of conflicting interests? What is it that the wise man knows? Let us listen to Koheles, the wisest of them all:

בקש קהלת למצא דברי חפץ וכתוב ישר דברי אמת.
Koheles would much rather have told you what you want to hear, but for honest writing there is nothing but the truth.

דברי חכמים כדרבנות וכמשמרות נטועים בעלי אספות נתנו מרעה אחד.
The words of the wise are like goads; they embed themselves like nails. The wise are masters of eclectic knowledge drawn from diverse sources which, in the end, all emanate from the One Shepherd.

ויתר מהמה בני הזהר עשות ספרים הרבה אין קץ ולהג הרבה יגעת בשר.
But, other than these, there is little point in writing endless books requiring constant study with no positive result other than draining one's strength.

סוף דבר הכל נשמע את האל־הים ירא ואת מצותיו שמור כי זה כל האדם.
For wisdom's final word, the sum of all possible truth is this: Fear God and live by His commandments. Nothing else really matters. (12:10–13)[11]

The words of the wise are like goads and nails. There is not much comfort there. They prod, they irk, they leave no rest. What, in the end, do they want from us?

They want us to grasp that life's experiences,[12] harsh and unreasonable as they may often seem, can all make us grow and gain wisdom. All of them are sent us by one loving and concerned Shepherd. And that makes all the difference. Shepherds love, shepherds nurture, and shepherds care only for their sheep. We may not always be able to understand, but we can always know that where the motivating energy is love, the end can only be good.

This is the wisdom of the truly wise.

Let us go back now to consideration of the verse with which we began our ruminations. God made man *yashar*, straight, but *heimah*—an unidentified "they" who turned away from the straightness with which God had endowed them—sought out *all kinds of complications*.

Yashrus dictates that there are not all kinds of complexities. Life in all its complexity is nothing more than a single light which expresses itself in the many colors of the rainbow after it is broken by the prism of the physical world which the loving Shepherd willed into being.

They were given by one Shepherd. That is the unifying theme, the *essence of things* of which the wise know. Once that is accepted as given, *all kinds of complications* lose their sting.

People

Man and Man

ALL OF US must deal with all kinds of people. That is a part of our lives which we simply cannot escape. Hillel HaZaken placed the ability and sensitivity needed for this most difficult of tasks at the very center of Judaism: Do not treat others in ways which you would consider hateful. That is the core. All else is no more than commentary to that basic, ineluctable concern (*Shabbos* 31a). So getting it right is very very important.

Getting it right, however, is not easy. Our deepest instincts balk at the idea that others have rights and feelings equal to our own. They set up a constant clamor that I and I and I and I and only I matter in any significant way. I am at the center and all else flows from that single relentless truth. That is simply the way we are. And what is more, our Sages recognized it. Why, they ask, was man, alone among God's creatures, created singly?[1] So that he might say, "It is for me that the world was created!" (*Sanhedrin* 37a)[2]

So now what? Now we need to think through how we are to steer our lives through the difficult and threatening shoals of human relationships.

What does Koheles say?

He seems to be intent upon offering middle-of-the-road guidance. Let us not be rigid, he says. There is a time for everything. There is a time to embrace and a time when it is better to maintain one's distance. Love and hatred each have their legitimate moments. War may be as valid an option as peace (3:5 and 8).

We need to keep our wits about us.

That, however, is not so easy. We all tend to react by instincts which are deeply ingrained—nurture and habit—instincts which importune us without much reference to any objective value system. Extraordinary discipline is required to exercise control over one's emotions, to be able to deal with relationships dispassionately and *halachically*. How can Koheles trust us so much? Are we really sufficiently good, sufficiently wise to be able to choose well between all the warring options?

Let us take one example of how, with gentle prodding, Koheles helps us do things right. How are we to deal with the fool? We all know how much and how severely he can provoke us. Koheles would suffer more than most. For him, wisdom stands at the very pinnacle of values and mere proximity to the fool must make him cringe. How does he approach the problem?

At first glance, Koheles seems to savage the fool mercilessly. With a deft flick of his dagger/pen, he seems to pillory him with devastatingly effective malice: "For like the crackle of thorns beneath the cauldron, so is the sound of the fool in his laughter" (7:6). The living picture leaps out at us from the page. The spectacle is as real as the writer's art can make it. Most of ours senses are inveigled into a feast of ridicule. We all but see the pitiful thorns yielding cravenly to the onslaught of the flames. We smell the acrid smoke and, cruelest touch of all, hear the meaningless crackle which grates so upon our nerves.

And yet, it is not really so at all. Only the spiritually tone-deaf would read with such crass insensitivity. Koheles demands better of his readers. He trusts us not to skim, but to open our hearts and minds to the aching pathos which animates this moving passage.

Why do just the useless thorns make so much noise? What inner need asserts itself through that ridiculous posturing? It is the simplest and most basic of all drives. It is the craving for an identity, the need to matter, to count for something, to fight the smothering mass of anonymity which chokes the passive and the weak.

The thorns are fighting, bravely if pathetically, against the oblivion to which a cruel uncaring nature seems to have condemned them. It is not, after all, their fault that nature has left them un-endowed. And no more can the fool be held responsible for his folly. The thorns affirm the absolute value of life. They do so by being determined to share in it by whatever poor means are available to them. The chattering fool is asking no less. He wants to count and to be counted. We can admire his persistence while decrying the emptiness of this world.

That we have picked up a significant nuance is confirmed by the next verse:

כי העשק יהולל חכם ויאבד לב מתנה

For frustration drives the wise to distraction, wreaking havoc in a heart endowed [with wisdom].

The sense of the verse, as read by the commentators, is to excuse the wise from trying to reform the fool. The arguments with which such obtuse minds would counter even a well-meant rebuke, would tax the wise beyond the pale of reason. There is just so much that one may ask an intelligent person to endure.

That is all well and good. However, what is the meaning of *matanah, endowed,* in this verse? Even granting the interpretation of the commentators who show that the word can really hint at wisdom, there is still the matter of discovering why here, of all places, this unusual terminology is used. Why use *endowed* when "wisdom" would have served as well?

In the context of our analysis, the explanation is simple enough. Wisdom is a divine gift. It is to be savored, it must be nurtured and protected; but it bestows no innate superiority at all. Avoid confrontation with the fool if you must. What God has so lovingly granted you may not be carelessly dissipated. Do not, however, become arrogant. You did nothing to earn that with which you preen. It was God's gift to you. It could have as easily found its way to him whom you would now make the butt of your conceit.

Here we have the balance of which we spoke. Both the wise man and the fool are precious. Both, in their stubborn incompatibility, demand their due. The aimless prattle of the one must awaken compassion but never derision. Nevertheless, that compassion must not be allowed to compromise, if only for a moment, the precious luster of the other.

There is indeed a time for everything. Koheles trusts the God-fearing person to find his way.

Man and Woman

What of man and woman? What does Koheles have to say about their respective roles? This issue has moved high up on the agenda of modern concerns. We may applaud this overblown interest or we may regret it. But it is there. It is there and the question, for better or worse, has taken on an air of extreme urgency. Let us follow where the Torah leads us.

Over the centuries, society has botched things badly. Often enough, man has harnessed his woman animal-like to his wagon, denigrated and abused her, brutalized himself by turning her into a brute. At other times, in other places and other cultures, he has prostrated himself before her, investing her with an exalted standing which was unearned and, therefore, unreal and untrue. Both modes are stupid, pernicious and destructive.

The Torah has something quite different in mind …

לזאת יקרא אשה כי מאיש לקחה זאת

This one shall be called woman, for from man was this one taken.

Man (ish) and *woman (ishah)*: the latter is merely the feminine form of the former (Hirsch). Both are of equal value before God. Woman is neither to be degraded nor to be worshipped. Most particularly, she is not to be patronized.

Truth has a beauty and a simplicity all of its own. However, for our purpose it can be no more than a starting point for useful discussion. Equality of value does not, at the end of the day, imply a congruence of nature or function; and it is these factors which determine relationships and societal equilibrium. So we need to do some more analysis.

What does Koheles teach us? At first blush his ideas seem awfully negative. How else to describe,

אדם אחד מאלף מצאתי ואשה בכל אלה לא מצאתי

I have managed to find one man in a thousand, but not a single woman among them all (7:28)?

And what of,

ומצא אני מר ממות את האשה אשר היא מצודים וחרמים
לבה אסורים ידיה טוב לפני האל־הים ימלט ממנה

Woman, who is a snare, whose heart is a net, whose hands are shackles, I consider to be worse than death. Only one with whom God is pleased will escape her (7:26).

There is not much comfort here for the woman who knows, beyond all questioning, that she, as much as any man, is of infinite value. The deck really does seem stacked against her.

And yet, we have seen only half the picture. Koheles has some other thoughts to share with us:

ראה חיים עם אשה אשר אהבת ... כי היא חלקך בחיים

Make your life together with a woman whom you love—for that is your portion in life ... (9:9).

That, we must admit, sounds very different.

And there is more. Could King Solomon, who in *Mishlei* sang of the *woman of valor* and proclaimed that...*he who has found a wife has found the [ultimate] good* (*Mishlei* 18:22), have written those other grating and seemingly destructive verses?

For an explanation we should go to Maharal in *Pirkei Avos*. There the mishnah teaches: *Do not talk to women more than you must. Those who talk much to women bring evil upon themselves, lose out on Torah study and, in the end, Gehinnom will be their lot.*

What could this possibly mean? God forbid that any mishnah should imply that women are somehow prone to *Gehinnom* and that by spending time with them, man can be caught up in that devastation. Maharal explains as follows: The problem here lies not with woman as woman, but with the confusion of roles which may come about through excessive and inappropriate interaction with her. In the Torah's scheme of life, men and women are assigned different roles. Man is the active, the creative, the initiating partner; woman provides the nurturing framework which lends courage and focus and imbues life's struggle with meaning. His duty is to wrestle with Abaye and Rava late into the night; hers to wrestle with sleep so that she might comfort his exhaustion, might welcome him home with warmth and beauty. She is the mother, the *eim* (related to *im*, the indispensable though more passive, conditional); he, the father (*av* from *avah*, to crave), whose look is ever outwards and upwards (Hirsch). Her world is the more circumscribed, more attuned to depth than to distance, focused more on husband and child than on a beckoning and challenging world. His mode is that of conqueror and provider whose home is his base but not his world.

What tragedy, Maharal reads from our mishnah, if those qualities and those interests which are such an adornment to the woman in her function as master-builder of her home, encroach insidiously upon the man's world. They lull, they cramp, they shackle. They undermine the lust for learning.

They stunt the questing spirit which must know no peace, to which "home" must never be more than a haven for finding strength to go on and on and on, ever outwards, ever upwards.

Let us look once more at *Koheles* 7:26:

Woman who is a snare, whose heart is a net, whose hands are shackles, I consider to be worse than death. Only one with whom God is pleased will escape her.

Read in the light of what we have learned, that lesson is abundantly clear and says nothing at all that is derogatory about women. It does say something about the travesty of womanized man.

We must examine the verses which follow this one more closely in order to savor the precise meaning of Koheles's assertion; that though he found one man in a thousand to be worthy, he did not find a single woman among them. The precise nuance will become clear only if we consider the Hebrew. The phrase, *Koheles said*, introducing *I have managed to find…* is an anomaly, for the verb is in the feminine form. But why?

Koheles was a man, he was king over Jerusalem. Why should he be projected here as a woman? The problem can be stated in more comprehensive terms. The word *Koheles* itself is a feminine form (thus nouns with the *es* ending). If so, why is it used as a man's name throughout the *megillah*? And, given that it is, why should an exception be made here?

We suspect that the explanation is as follows: We have talked of men and women in absolute terms, as though all men were always so, all women always thus. But it is clear enough that in human nature there are precious few absolutes. Our reactions to the challenges which life hurls at us are always complex, often ambiguous. No woman is completely feminine, no man exclusively masculine. Women occasionally have to struggle with instincts which, if left unchecked, would drive them beyond the bounds of appropriate modesty. Men will sometimes feel locked into unfamiliar and threatening lethargy. It is with exquisite sensitivity that King Solomon gave his protagonist a feminine name but a masculine identity. By this stratagem, he conveyed to us that serving God out of fear, the subject of our megillah as we have so often stressed, can help us to find our true selves beneath the occasional lapses which confuse and dispirit us. Be serious, he is telling us, and the aberrant weaknesses within us will not matter. Koheles, with all the feminine inclinations implied in the name, can be king of Jerusalem.

What, then, of the unexpected feminine verb of our verse?[3]

It seems obvious that King Solomon's cry of despair, the sorry discovery that only one in a thousand can be said to have succeeded, was uttered in a moment of personal weakness. Koheles, the feminine within him, had come to the fore and he felt himself remiss, felt that he was falling short of the accomplishments which he had learned to demand of himself. He traced his failure to his weakness in allowing the feminine within himself to dominate.

In that moment of despair, he looked around and realized that there were only so few, so very few, who could really be said to have gone all the way. And this he ascribed to the very weakness which he had only now discovered within himself.[4]

This is the true meaning of the statement, *but not a single woman among them all*. Not one of all those who had really succeeded had allowed his feminine instincts to control him. All had been faithful to their true nature.

*   *   *

Bava Basra 16b commiserates with those whose children are females. That sentiment, can, of course, be understood as maintaining that it is better to have sons than to have daughters. But the language is pliable enough to allow for another interpretation:

אוי לו למי שבניו נקבות

How sad for him whose sons are females, who have fallen victim to the feminine instincts which are a part of their humanity (see Meiri at the end of Kiddushin).

מה יתרון לאדם בכל עמלו שיעמול תחת
השמש

*What benefit does man have from all his labor
if he invests his energies beneath the sun?
(1:3)*

ראה חיים עם אשה אשר אהבת כל ימי חיי
הבלך אשר נתן לך תחת השמש כל ימי הבלך
כי הוא חלקך בחיים ובעמלך אשר אתה עמל
תחת השמש

*Make sure that throughout the life of futility
which [God] assigned to you beneath the sun,
you establish life with a wife with whom you
have found love. That alone is your portion
in life and [the justification or the profit] of
all the labor which you invest beneath the
sun. (9:9)*

Man and Wife

T HERE IS nothing quite like marriage.

This is not a very profound statement. Few people
would quarrel with it.[5] But King Solomon, in *Koheles* or anywhere else, does not deal with the bland bromides of everyday
convention. So what precisely is being said in the second of
the two quotes which we set at the head of this chapter? We
will need some very careful analysis.

Let us begin by placing the two passages next to one another.

הבל הבלים
אמר קוהלת,
הבל הבלים
הכל הבל. מה
יתרון לאדם
בכל עמלו
שיעמול תחת
השמש.

Vanity of vanities, said Koheles. Vanity of vanities, everything is vanity.

לך אכול בשמחה לחמך ושתה בלב טוב יינך כי כבר
רצה האל־הים את מעשך. בכל עת יהיו בגדיך לבנים
ושמן על ראשך אל יחסר. ראה חיים עם אשה אשר
אהבת כל ימי **חיי הבלך** אשר נתן לך **תחת השמש** כל
ימי הבלך כי הוא חלקך בחיים ובעמלך **אשר אתה עמל
תחת השמש.** כל אשר תמצא ידך לעשות בכחך עשה
כי אין מעשה וחשבון ודעת וחכמה בשאול אשר אתה
הולך שמה.

Go eat your bread in joy and drink your wine with a good heart, for God has already seen your deed. At all times, let your garments be white and do not lack oil upon your head. Make your life together with the woman whom you love all the days of your life of vanity, which He has given you under the sun, all the days of your vanity, for that is your portion in life and in your toil in which you engage under the sun. All that you find your hand able to do, do, for there is no deed and accounting and knowledge and wisdom in Sheol, to which you are going.

How are we to make peace between these two radically different perceptions of life beneath the sun? What has happened to the stark pessimism of the earlier quote?

Now it is certainly true that much of the bleakness with which Koheles seems to have viewed existence initially later gives way to a more positive, life-embracing posture. We chart this progress in a number of our essays and, as we demonstrate in *Celebrating Life*, the penultimate essay in this little book, it seems to be just this movement from negation to affirmation which energizes the entire megillah.

In our passage, however, nothing of this change of heart seems to be operative. So that we make no mistake at all about its agreement with the negativism of the earlier verse, we twice have *vanity* as the central reality of life (*all the days of your life of vanity* and *all the days of your vanity*), and the *toil* which occupies us is one which is directed *under the sun*. The language in Chapter 9 clearly and consistently echoes the earlier verse with its focus on *vanity* and *under the sun*. There can be no doubt at all, then, that we are meant to make an association between the two.

So we make the association. And then, what? Then we find ourselves in a new world. Sober optimism replaces the hopelessness of the past. Even in life lived *under the sun*, there can be solid, satisfying accomplishments. Even in a life of vanity lived in the glare of the sun, it is possible to find a meaningful place for oneself.

Everything is in apparent total contradiction to what we have learned before of the absolute and hopeless futility of things. What has happened? Koheles has discovered a secret. A wife whom we have learned to love can make all the difference. How may she do this? She can point to a way that leads out of the inhibiting shackles which are the characteristics of a vain existence lived under the dazzling sun. She can take us by the hand and lead us into the shade.

We go back to the very first moment in which woman makes her appearance. God has paraded all the animals in front of Adam so that he might assign names to them. He delves deeply into their essence and function in order to determine their appropriate place in the world which he has now been called upon to harness to his service.

He understands them all, names them all, but cannot find a single one which could be called a *helpmeet*—an *ezer kenegdo*—literally, *helper neged him. Neged* always describes a relationship. It carries many different denotations. These include: in the presence of, opposite, over against, towards, and the like.[6] An *eizer kenegdo* would be a helpmate with whom he could live in a meaningful relationship. In the animal world, Adam found many creatures that could be described as a helper, but none at all who could help him by serving as a companion.

There was no commonality between them. He could never recognize himself in them; therefore, the names that he assigned to them could never be derived from his own. Then God fashioned the woman. And Adam called out in wonderment: *This one shall be called woman, for from man was this one taken! (Bereishis* 2:23).[7]

This was not only a *helper*, but one that could stand *kenegdo*. For the first time, Adam was able to look outside himself and beyond himself. Till this moment, he only had seen creatures that he could control. He had stood as an exploiter vis-à-vis the world, albeit perhaps a benign one. He owed no one a reckoning. Nothing was barred to him if he only had the strength or cunning to take it.

Suddenly he beholds an equal; one to whom the physical world is as subservient as it is to him. One whom he must consider and with whom he must reach an accommodation. One for whom he must care and with whom caring could turn to love.

And, wonder of wonders, it is in that moment that *Adam*, the earth-man,[8] turns into *ish*, the aristocrat, the master.[9] The *ish* discovers himself in the *ishah*. He looks at his wife and finds nobility within himself.[10]

We return to our passage in *Koheles*. There is, King Solomon tells us, a way out from the futility of a life in which all effort is directed beneath the sun. Find a wife whom you are able to love and the chances are that you will have discovered the portion that may still redeem you from the abyss into which you have allowed yourself to sink.[11] By being forced to allow another to matter, you will of necessity be looking beyond yourself. And once your look is directed outwards, you may yet discover the world above the sun.

Friends

WE ARE NEVER MORE SOLITARY than when we move among people with whom we can feel no sense of kinship. We are never more despairing than when society fails us and we find ourselves, with people all around us, to be utterly alone. We need friends and it is not easy to find them. We crave the company of good people and they are hard to come by.

It is the terrifyingly predatory nature of man which brings Koheles to his lowest moment:

Observing once more, I saw all the victims under the sun. Here were the tears of the downtrodden that have no one at all to comfort them. Their oppressors have power, but for them there is no comfort. And so, I considered those who had already died as luckier than those who were still living. More fortunate than both—he who has not yet been born, who had not at all witnessed all the evil that was perpetrated under the sun (4:1–3).

The facts, sadly enough, are clear and undeniable. But Koheles insists on delving beneath the surface. What makes people so unpleasant? Why is society, taken as a whole, such an abysmal failure? He has the answer:

*I realized that so much labor, so much ingenuity
was driven by no more than jealousy between men...
(4:4).*

Nothing at all has changed from the earliest dawn of human experience. The centuries might as well not have passed, the toils and sorrows which bled poor suffering history white, might as well have been spared. Humanity had not progressed one whit beyond that first dreadful moment when Cain, crazed by that selfsame lust for self-assertion which Shlomo is now bemoaning, sullied the pristine earth with Hevel's blood.

It is easy to understand why, among the human failings which Koheles pillories with such vehemence, it is man's propensity to self-aggrandizement which most disturbs him. Of all our shortcomings, it is this one which stands most blatantly in opposition to *hachna'ah*, the posture of submission which is the hallmark of the *avodah miyir'ah* to which he has devoted this megillah.

What to do?

הכסיל חובק את ידיו ואכל את בשרו

*The fool folds his hands, thereby consuming his own
flesh. (4:5)*

The sensitive soul withdraws, turtle-like, into itself. Pessimism is fertile ground for the isolationism of the spirit.

Note well, however. The person who acts that way is a fool. His perceptions are all wrong. We cannot cut ourselves off from our community any more than we can deny our own selves. Whether we like it or not, we are a part of society and it is a part of us. As the starving body ultimately gnaws away at its own flesh, pathetically attempting to find within itself the resources which so patently must come from others, so must we, in isolation, destroy ourselves.

It is foolish to be a fool.

Well and good. It seems that we are fated to travel through life together. Clearly, then, there must be ways of coping. It is inconceivable that God would wish us to be swept up and carried away by the passions which evidently animate the corrupt society which Koheles had earlier described and decried.

Koheles has a suggestion: The secret lies in winning emancipation from, of all people, ourselves. The "I" will always crave more; the "we" has a chance of assuaging its thirst.

ושבתי אני ואראה הבל תחת השמש. יש אחד ואין שני גם בן ואח אין לו ואין קץ לכל עמלו גם עינו לא תשבע עשר ולמי אני עמל ומחסר את נפשי מטובה. גם זה הבל וענין רע הוא.

Once more I became frustrated by what I observed under the sun. There may be a person utterly alone, who has neither son nor brother, whose exertions are without end, whose ambitions are never quieted by fulfillment. For whom then do I labor denying myself pleasure. This too is futility, a terrible thing! (4:6–8)

This is an eye-opener. Man does, after all, have something over the animal world. He does not relish the prospect of working for himself alone. Pleasure in his accomplishments is incomplete if he cannot share the fruits of his labor with another.

This idea is so radical that Koheles teases it gingerly, approaches it with reserve, savors it first as an objective truth, in the third person (*there is a lone person*), and only then permits himself to internalize it and have it true for his own life (*for whom do I labor*).

Carefully Koheles moves on to a contemplation of the truth which he has now uncovered. In a world purposefully created, such instincts cannot be without purpose. What advantages accrue to us from our instinctive flight from solitude? His analysis will uncover insights of which, at the start of his intellectual travels, he could have known nothing.

טובים השנים מן האחד... כי אם יפלו...
…Two are better than one… for if they were to fall…
(4:9–10)

Initially he sees our instinct for companionship as purely utilitarian. We need someone to help us up after a fall, a supporting arm in the time of our vulnerability. It is clear that we cannot make it on our own. But this paradigm is still a very primitive one. It perceives one's fellow as object rather than subject, as someone to be used rather than someone with whom to share life.

גם אם ישכבו שנים וחם להם ולאחד איך יחם.
Furthermore, two who lie together feel warm. But how can one person by himself find comfort? (4:11)

Once embarked upon this path of discovery, Koheles finds that there is no way back. Insight begets insight, experience cradles wisdom in its embrace. The next stage follows inevitably upon the first. If it is true that my friend can help me up after a fall, it is equally true that I can render him the same service. He and I are two of the same, two limbs of one body, two ideas animating one another. We can lie in each other's arms, warming and sustaining. Taking becomes giving, giving becomes a feast of love, a feast of sharing. Koheles has found a friend.

ואם יתקפו האחד השנים יעמדו נגדו...
Now if the one were attacked, the two could stand up against him (4:12).

Friendship, Koheles learns, ennobles. Friends sacrifice for friends. When one is attacked both are the victims. They are willing to take up cudgels for one another because they have learned that they are ultimately one.

What of the last cryptic phrase in this passage? What is this *three-stranded thread which cannot be quickly broken*? Is there, then, a perception of society which carries us beyond the enlightened vision which has even now inspired us?

Apparently, there is, and it delights in its simplicity. Fellowship is its own reward. It requires no justification. The third man, whose hand is not required to lift the fallen, whose warmth need quicken no freezing body, whose weapons repulse no enemy because there are sufficient forces without him, is the one in whom Koheles recognizes the ultimate value of the Other. As long as we are in the "two-mode," as long as human value is measured in utilitarian terms, the thread that joins us can readily be broken. Postulate self-sufficiency and the desert island will serve as well as the village square. It is a sorry world indeed in which, because I have no need of your help, I have no need of you!

It is only with the appearance of a third, apparently superfluous presence, that Koheles learns what really animates our relationships. We are, he discovers, very different from the animals. We value people not for what they do, but for what they are. We form bonds because we want to be bonded. We need not be shackled by myopic self-absorption. We can vacate the center of our little personal fiefdoms and move to the side. We can look beyond ourselves and, wonder of wonders, behold a man! He is one who owes me no explanations, no excuses. He is because he is, even as I am because I am, and he is one whom I treasure because he Is!

Money

Wealth

WE ALL WANT IT. FOR some of us the craving is more insistent, for others less so, but all of us, at some level, want it. The prayer with which we usher in Rosh Chodesh captures our longings precisely. With no less fervor than we invest in begging God to help us fear Him and love His Torah, we also ask Him for *a life brightened by wealth*[1] *and the respect of our peers*. There it is; a basic and universal need. Money is *kesef*, from *kasef*, to long for, to crave. It is that which we want very, very much. We might accurately translate the word as simply, tangible desire. If we are human it is important to us. That is just the way we are.

But is it the way we should be?

Let us analyze the issues squarely and honestly. Koheles will surprise us. Not all our weaknesses are as bad as we might suppose. We are neither as guilty as our overloaded consciences would have us fear, nor as unblemished as we would wish to be. Money is dynamite. It will not leave us untouched. One way or another we must deal with it. But there are ways that are better than others. How can we do it best?

Come let us learn.

THE DOWN SIDE

We know what the lust for money can do to us:

> *Observing once more, I saw all the victims under the sun. Here were the tears of the downtrodden who have no one at all to comfort them. Their oppressors have power—but for them there is no comfort. And so I considered those who had already died as luckier than those who were still living. More fortunate than both—he who has not yet been born, who has not at all witnessed all the evil that is perpetrated under the sun (4:1–3).*

It is a horrible picture. It is money that drives ambition. Money and the power which comes wrapped in it.

But even without any special propensity towards evil, money can still corrode and corrupt. There is no escaping its allure, no denying its pull. That is what Koheles tells us in 5:8: *All are held in thrall by the land; even the king is servant to the farmer.* This is the bitter reality. We all need bread. And most of us will do anything, truly anything, to obtain it.

Earlier, King Solomon spelled it out:

אם עשק רש וגזל משפט וצדק תראה במדינה אל תתמה
על החפץ...

If you come across a society in which the poor are oppressed, and justice and righteousness have been spirited away, it should not at all surprise you… (5:7)

Society is predatory. There is a constant struggle for security which in people's minds can be assured only by ascendancy. Because we must eat. It is as simple as that.

THE BEGINNINGS OF A SOLUTION

What to do? Do we really need to accept a state of eternal

strife and back-biting as a given? Is there no escape from the jungle?

Koheles has some advice for us: *If you love money you will never get enough of it, and one whose satisfaction lies only in abundance, will never know the joys of a harvest* (5:9).

Try not to become enamored of wealth. It is true that you need it, but it is equally true that you need not love it. Excess is the illegitimate offspring of misplaced love.

One can accept this. It can even bring some tranquility to our lives. But a question remains. Why did God imbue us with this unending appetite? Are we fated to forever torture ourselves with frustrated longings which can never be assuaged? Is that really what God wants?

Not at all, says R' Tzadok HaKohen of Lublin (*Yisrael Kedoshim*, p. 13, #25). Our persistent and unremitting cravings were given us to be a function of our better selves. Our striving for the sacred, the uplifting, the edifying, can never, nor should we ever want it to be, satisfied. It summons us to another more worthwhile world, *the true portion of Jacob, which is totally without boundaries.* It is only in its corrupted form, when we prostitute it to make wealth and power its focus, that it becomes the scourge which turns every joy to bitterness, every accomplishment to disillusion.

Our Sages have a story to tell. They attached it to 6:7.

כל עמל האדם לפיהו וגם הנפש לא תמלא

Let all man's labor be undertaken only that there might be sufficient food for his mouth, for the soul's cravings will never be satisfied.

Here's the story:

A villager married a princess. In an attempt to make her happy, he brought her the choicest delicacies which he could find. All she did was to pout. There was nothing he could do to satisfy her. She was, after all, a princess. The palace could and did provide her with anything she wanted. From her husband she needed something else.

The same is true of the soul. Since it comes from heaven it will spurn even the greatest luxury which our poor world has to offer. It seeks fulfillment in a very different currency (*Koheles Rabba*).

You must give up the struggle for ever more and ever greater wealth because there is absolutely no way of winning. Moreover, if you want to be able to enjoy your harvest, you must understand the dynamics of satisfaction. It does not follow from a bulging silo. There will always be a neighbor who does better. Abundance can never be the true measure of accomplishment. It all appears niggardly next to someone who has more.

Does this mean that we will never be able to enjoy the fruits of our labor? Not at all!

הנה אשר ראיתי אני, טוב אשר יפה לאכול ולשתות ולראות טובה בכל עמלו שיעמל תחת השמש מספר ימי חיו אשר נתן לו האל־הים כי הוא חלקו.

See now, this is my personal observation: It is good, even beautiful, to eat, drink and feel good about the labor which he has performed beneath the sun, throughout the life which God has granted him, for this is his portion (5:17).

Labor can be its own reward.[2] So it is not as large a problem as we thought. We can extricate ourselves from the downward spiral of being either the oppressor or the oppressed. Neither of these two are what we should want to be, neither are what God wants us to be. The secret lies in control, in directing our love where it belongs, in learning to find satisfaction in the truly satisfying.

Effort is its own reward. Its measure is the feeling of duty conscientiously rendered, never the dubious victories in the battle of the bushels.

* * *

But is this all? Is a world in which money energizes all the machinery only something which we can learn to live with, or does it contain something more positive for us? We will take this question up in the next chapter.

Labor

Let us study a bit of *Tehillim*:

> *You call forth darkness and night falls; time for every forest beast to stir. Lions roar for prey, asking for their food from God. As the sun rises their homes reclaim them, they settle down in their lair. Now man goes forth to his work, to labor until the evening. (Tehilim 104:20–23)*

This passage is followed immediately by David's jubilant proclamation:

How great are Your creations, Hashem! How much wisdom have You invested in every one of them! (*Tehillim* 104:24)

Man's labor, then, is a wonderful thing. It takes its place among the glories of nature of which Psalm 104 sings. It too testifies to the wisdom which God has lavished on creation. It harmonizes with the myriad notes which together form the music which a world of purpose and harmony offers to its Creator.

This lyric accolade to labor is reflected in the *Shulchan Aruch*. After exhorting us to assign a fixed time for learning in the morning, the *halachah* continues: *After he has learned*

Torah... let him go attend to his business. Torah unaccompanied by work will in the end be useless, bringing sin in its wake. Poverty breeds rebellion against God's wishes ... (Orach Chaim 156:1).[3]

OF MEN AND LIONS

Let us submit the *Tehillim* passage to a closer reading. Ponder the difference between the lion and the man. The lion's mode is the night, his focus is entirely upon his sustenance, and his efforts are limited to seeking God's bounty through his roar. The mode of man is the day. Without any apparent reference to God, he labors long and hard until evening. There is no indication at all as to what the object of his labor might be. We may assume what we may. For the psalmist, the matter seems to be of no significance.

NIGHT AND DAY

Night is the time when nature is quiescent. It is the time of miracles.[4] Human activity comes to an end and God is very close. All of nature is passive: the activity of the beasts of prey is itself a kind of passivity. They roar out their wants and God, as it were, answers their call and supplies their need.

By day, nature comes into its own. God is hidden behind a maelstrom of apparently autonomous activity. Man, and man's ability to fend for himself, to build, to produce, holds center stage. He acts as sovereign, owing no one any explanation. He goes off to work and returns home at night. His motives are his own business. What ideas should energize us as we go about our daily tasks?

THE PLAY'S THE THING

Now I developed a hatred for all the labor which I invested beneath the sun—for I would have to leave it to whomever would follow me. Who knows whether he will be wise or foolish—but either way he will control all the labor which I invested and upon which I lavished so much wisdom. This too is vanity (2:18–19).

Koheles raises an important question here. How are we to look upon our efforts to make a living, to contribute, positively we hope, to society? To what extent should we identify with the houses which we build, the bridges through which we beat distance into submission, the businesses in which we invest so much creativity, the brews in our laboratories, the spread-sheets in our computers? Are they meaningless in terms of our striving to live our lives as servants of God; or is there a place in Judaism for the love which we tend to feel for the ordinary and the familiar, for our desks and our carpools, for the physical props which dot the stage upon which the drama of our lives unfolds?

The question centers upon a correct understanding of God's blessing to the male and female whom He created. *Fill the earth and make your mark upon it* (literally, *conquer it*) (*Bereishis* 1:28). Ramban explains that we conquer the earth to the extent that we force it to yield its bounty. All that the earth has to offer is ours. We are to mine its treasures, to uncover its secrets and to unleash its energies. It is God's gift; the opportunity which He has handed us so that we might join Him in creative and constructive effort.

What are we to make of this blessing? Are we indeed to be intimately involved in the development of our world? Does it have a legitimate claim upon our attention and energies because it is ours and it is right that we should care about it? Or do we forever remain strangers in this paradise, functioning in it because such is God's will, but never really being part of it?

A case can be made that we must distinguish between Israel and the gentile peoples. There are differences in roles and therefore differences in legitimate aspirations. Let us examine the context in which God's gift of conquest was made.

It seems boundlessly significant that it is recorded in the earlier creation narrative in which the first humans are as yet without name. Here they function only as male and female; not until the second chapter do Adam and Chavah assume identity and individualism. This may well support our thesis. The duty to develop the earth as an objective value devolves upon those who constitute the masses of humanity. These are differentiated only in their gender. Adam and Chavah, the strivers[5] and the educators,[6] have a different agenda.[7]

This distinction between Jew and gentile was later institutionalized by Yitzchak in the blessings which he gave to his two sons Yaakov and Eisav. Yaakov was granted the bounties of this world only to the extent that they would contribute to his spiritual growth. Eisav received them with absolutely no conditions attached (See Rashi, *Bereishis* 27:28). Yaakov's element is the world-to-come. He relates to this world as one does to an antechamber. Whatever does not contribute to his entry into the palace has no meaning for him. For Eisav, the antechamber is the palace. It is his only reality.

Let us return to the object of Koheles's hatred. How dreadful, he muses, that those causes, legitimate or questionable, to which we have given our best efforts, may end up under the control of an incompetent fool who will quickly destroy all that we have built up with so much love and dedication?

But note well! The question is introduced with a caveat. Koheles hates life because that which he has observed *under the sun,* is distasteful to him. The implication is clear enough. One must have an attitude that is not cramped by a life lived beneath the sun. We must develop an attitude with which we can cope constructively with such potential frustrations.

And indeed there is; for us, for Israel, for whom the world is the antechamber, but never the palace. If the construction and development of the physical world is not an end in itself, but has significance only to the extent that it facilitates passage from the antechamber to the palace, then the definition of success or failure undergoes subtle change. The bridge which I build may do its job in an exemplary manner and may yet be counted as a dead loss. The objective world has been substantially improved, but my inner world may have been shattered. The construction may have been an activity in which I should not have engaged. Conversely, the bridge may never carry a single traveler and yet, if God was well-pleased with the effort which I invested, I will, while building it, have lived positively and constructively.

There is nothing better for man than to eat and drink and permit himself to rejoice *in his labors. For it is clear to me that this too is a gift from God* (2:24). Here we have the answer. We are to rejoice, not in the tangible success of the venture, but in the labor which attended it.

An entirely new, entirely positive attitude towards life's tasks now emerges. Protected from the fears and frustrations which are the necessary attendants of objective goals, a *joie de vivre* becomes possible which results in an enthusiastic shouldering of effort and involvement. Where the prospect of failure holds no terrors, no one will seek to procrastinate or dawdle. Koheles waxes positively lyrical in his praise of the committed laborer:

Sloth will cause the ceiling to disintegrate; the house where hands hang idle will drip with water (10:18).

He who waits for a fair wind will never sow; he who watches the clouds will never reap (11:4).

Sow your seeds in the morning, but do not rest in the evening; for you know not whether these or those will turn out well, or whether perhaps both will be good. How sweet the light! How good for the eyes to behold

*the sun! For even if man were to live for many years,
let him rejoice in all of them. And let him remember
the days of darkness for they will be many indeed …*
(11:6–8).

The message is clear: Life is sweet. Make the most of it!
By appropriating the correct perspective, one may accomplish a reordering of priorities. Ends are downgraded into means, the fires of ambition are banked and despair makes room for hope. We are freed from the corroding naggings of frustration because all effort, so long as it is undertaken honestly, responsibly and for the right reasons, will inevitably be crowned by success.

Shadows

Of Goodness and Beauty

L ET US THINK a little more about wealth. Most of us spend much of our time trying to make a living. It pays to have a clear perception of the rights and wrongs of the matter.

Pirkei Avos (2:2) teaches that *there is a special beauty in the combination of Torah and derech eretz.* What precisely is *derech eretz*? And why is its combination with Torah so beautiful?

We will take Rambam's interpretation as our point of departure. *Derech eretz* is simply working at making a living. *Midrash Rabba*, and the Vilna Gaon as well, appear to agree with Rambam. As the source for the mishnah's contention, they offer *Koheles* 7:11: *Wisdom is good when it is combined with possessions.*

So why *beauty?* Why not retain the *good* of the *Koheles* passage? Why not, *it is good to have a combination of Torah and derech eretz?*[1] Let us see what lies beneath the change.

The mishnah in *Avos* continues with an explanation: *because energetic involvement with both Torah and labor leaves no room for sin.* Given the midrash's assertion that the first part of the mishnah is based on *Koheles*, it seems reasonable to expect that the ending of the mishnah can be found there too. Can our megillah be adduced as a source for this reasoning also?

The best place to look would certainly be the same verse. Accordingly, we should move to the end of 7:11, *and an advantage to those who look upon the sun,* and examine its precise meaning.

CASTING SHADOWS—
ESCAPING THE GLARE OF THE SUN

Who are these people who look upon the sun?

In Endnote #2 in the chapter entitled *Finding Joy in Unlikely Places,* we analyzed the concept of the sun and found that the sun, source of energy and life on earth, is the Torah's preeminent metaphor for the "this-worldly" and the temporal. On the basis of this insight, we argued that the ubiquitous *under the sun* as it appears in *Koheles,* would be that state in which all those aspects of life which so dissatisfy Koheles, would flourish. Indeed, there is very little to be said for a society which conducts its affairs *under the sun.*

If we accept this, however, what are we to make of 11:7, which seems to turn the entire thesis on its head? There, in the context of a lyric description of the need to plunge into the demands and challenges of daily life with enthusiasm and vigor, we read:

ומתוק האור וטוב לעינים לראות את השמש
How sweet is the light! How good it is for the eyes to behold the sun!

Good to behold the sun? The very villain of *under the sun?* What has happened?

It is the subtle change in wording which makes all the difference. The phrase *under the sun* carries the connotation of being beneath the sun and thus under its influence and control. That is bad, very bad. *To look upon the sun* implies objective evaluation undertaken by one who remains on the outside, insists on being master of his own destiny. It implies one who does nothing except for that which his own good sense finds beneficial. From such a vantage point, with autonomy unimpaired, one can observe the "sun" and find it good and sweet.

This sentence puts all that we have learned before into a new perspective. The sun, after all, is not as bad as we had thought. Subordinate yourself under its influence, and you create a life of vanity. Maintain unfettered independence, shrug off its pernicious and diminishing control, and you may bask in its benign warmth.

Those who look upon the sun are the heroic figures who have fought long and hard to extricate themselves from the shackling smallness of the *under the sun* mode. They are the ones whom God can trust, to whom the inheritance is of boundless advantage. It is for them, and them alone, that the combination of wisdom and wealth is a priceless boon. They are in control. They are not threatened by, nor need they fear, the *kisufin = kesef, longing = silver*[2] allures which make such shambles of the resolutions of lesser men. For such as these, *derech eretz* is indeed the perfect adornment for Torah.

Why? Because, as the next verse makes clear, *under the shadow of wisdom, money too can provide shade.* Because with the right attitudes and the requisite discipline, money can protect from sin as surely and efficiently as wisdom can.

It is all a matter of granting freedom from the tyranny of the sun. It is a matter of providing shade. Wisdom clearly furnishes an effective canopy. Within that canopy, money too has an invaluable role to play.

We quote *Koheles Rabba* together with the comments of the immortal R' Yitzchak Z'ev Yadler:

ד"א טובה חכמה כשיש עמה נחלה

Wisdom is good only when it is combined with possessions.[3]

Rav Yadler comments: because he has possessions, his mind is at peace, and this enables him to concentrate on his learning. But one who does not have adequate income can never concentrate sufficiently because he is constantly worried about making a living. This is what R' Yehudah meant when he said: If my wallet is lost, my heart is lost.[4]

Money handled correctly casts the same blessed shade as wisdom.

BEAUTY IN ACTION

Here, then, we have real loveliness, *beautiful* replacing *good*. What is beauty, after all, if not the artful interplay between disparate elements which the master's hand can conjure up from deep within his creative soul? It is the unexpected harmony between potentially warring entities which delights the eye and elevates the spirit.

What can be more beautiful than the integrated personality balancing the eternal with the temporal, bringing the one down to earth,[5] raising the other up to heaven,[6] and creating paradise in the present tense.

BUT THERE ARE PRIORITIES

There is integrity, there is balance and there is beauty. None of these, however, suggest absolute equality. Wisdom may indeed be adorned by possessions, but it is no more than an adornment. Wisdom always retains its dominance. It is ultimately the only one of the two that really matters.

Thus Koheles:

... ויתרון דעת החחכמה תחיה בעליה

... but knowledge remains preeminent. It is only wisdom that grants [meaningful] life (7:12).

SOME CONCLUSIONS

In the previous chapter, we learned what a difference a correct attitude can make. We saw how it can eliminate frustrations, turn fears into fulfillment, arid hopelessness into joyful affirmation.

In this chapter, we went one step further. The pursuit of possessions is not only a necessary evil, albeit one amenable to sublimation, but a positive and indispensable part of living the life envisaged by the Torah. It is an adornment to wisdom, absent which, except under the most special of circumstances, the beauty of the completed and integrated personality would be diminished.

BUT ...

Nevertheless, and this we must remember, it is only for those who look upon the sun, only for the heroes among us.

THE DAY AND
THE MEGILLAH

הבל הבלים... הכל הבל. מה יתרון לאדם בכל
עמלו שיעמל תחת השמש.
*Be aware of life's utter futility[1] ... hevel is all-
pervasive. What, after all, can man hope to
gain by all his labors when these are directed
to life beneath the sun. (1:2)*

טוב ללכת אל בית אבל מלכת אל בית משתה
באשר הוא סוף כל האדם, והחי יתן אל לבו.
*Far better to frequent the mourner's house
than to spend time in partying. Death, after
all, is everyone's lot, and the living would do
well to ponder this. (7:2)*

כי אם שנים הרבה יחיה האדם בכלם ישמח ויזכר
את ימי החשך כי הרבה יהיו כל שבא הבל.
*If a man be granted many years, let him fill
every one of them with joy. But let him also
remember the days of darkness that lie ahead.
There will be many of them. [Only] those days
that are yet to come are hevel. (11:8)*

Celebrating Life

WE HAVE QUOTED the three passages which, taken
together, might be said to anchor King Solomon's
ruminations on the meaning of life. The first and last respectively begin and end his thoughts. The middle one might be
viewed as serving to bridge the two.

The first and final quotes could hardly be more antithetical to one another. There is a world of difference between seeing vanity as the pervasive reality of all life on earth and relegating it to the infinity beyond the grave. The lines are sharply drawn. Between the beginning of the megillah and its end, Koheles has become convinced that life in this world can be very good indeed. The bleak pessimism of the early chapters has given way to a jubilant affirmation of life.

The key to the change is stated plainly enough in the third of our quotes: *But let him also remember the days of darkness that lie ahead.* This, of course, is the identical thought which was expressed in our bridge passage: *Death, after all, is everyone's lot, and the living would do well to ponder this.*

Life is transient. There is just no comparison between the time we spend on earth and the infinity of the beyond. We need to worry more about an endless future than about a paltry present. Koheles has discovered fear.

It is all a matter of perception. Life as self-validating, as filling the entire canvas of experience, as being therefore an address from which all kinds of gratification can be expected and demanded, can never be more than a jumble of frustrations and disappointments. However, if we look at it as a short interlude between birth and oblivion, a time for hoarding constructive experiences against an existence in which absolutely no growth will be possible any longer, it becomes another matter altogether. Every moment becomes an opportunity for creative and productive activity; the most mundane task summons us to joy and unbounded enthusiasm.

Mark time waiting for a fair wind—and you will never sow. Be scared of any little cloud and you will never reap... Sow your seeds in the morning, but even as evening comes, do not stand idle. You can never know for sure whether your earlier or your later efforts will be more successful. It could be that both might be equally

*good. How sweet light can be, how good the sight of
the sun for the eyes. If a man be granted many years,
let him fill every one with joy… (11:4–12:7)*

What a paean to life we have here! How different from the
gloom of the earlier chapters which saw only vanity, vanity
and more vanity.

Koheles has discovered a sparkling world of hope and
promise. His sights have moved from beneath the sun to a
beyond which lends perspective and balance to the endless
complexities which had troubled him so much. There are not
many answers, but there are fewer questions. Experiences
have turned from ends to means; the focus has moved from
the Self to the Other.

Koheles has entered the world of the *succah* as we recognized it in our opening chapter, *Shelter in the Shade*. He has
found protection from the glaring sun.

Shadows Under the Eaves

Succos, of course, is only part of the story. Its lessons would remain incomplete if they would have to stand on their own. Succos flows into and culminates with Shemini Atzeres and only then achieves its realization and completion.[2] It is strange but true. Succos, the holiday with more mitzvah objects than any other, finds its highest and deepest expression in a day which eschews absolutely any and all concretization.[3] What could this possibly mean?

The absence of any tangible symbols makes it very clear that Shemini Atzeres wishes us to *be* rather than to *do*, to relate to God rather than to serve Him.

It is inevitable that there should be such a day. The *succah*, after all, is no more than a temporary structure. It is with us a mere seven days and unless somehow preserved, its gifts would slip into history, becoming precious memories with no lasting impact upon our lives. That simply cannot be. It cannot be that God would want to grant us the heady experience of life lived in His presence and then have it all sink into oblivion. Shemini Atzeres is there to guarantee continuity. It is the day on which we, so to speak, bring the *succah* into our house. What was accomplished for the past seven days when we felt so close to God under the shadow of the flimsy thatch *s'chach*, must now be matched under the eaves. That is a lot harder. The ordinary and mundane must be made to cradle sanctity. The very essence of the day's glory is expressed in the absence of any symbols. On Shemini Atzeres we are summoned to greatness as we are. We stand or fall on our own. We must, as we noted above, *be* rather than *do*.

And on Shemini Atzeres we celebrate Simchas Torah. Why?

Because, on such a day, we rejoice in that which gives us our character. We rejoice in that which forms and nurtures us into people. We rejoice that we are a people who can rise to such an awesome challenge. The poet got it right:

נגיל ונשיש בזאת התורה כי היא עוז ואורה

Let us exult and rejoice with this Torah for it *[and it alone] is our strength and light. (Machzor Simchas Torah)*

There we have it. Shemini Atzeres would be nothing at all without the Torah. It is that and only that which makes us what we are.

*   *   *

We return to Koheles and find our ideas confirmed.

In our earlier essay, *Shadows*, we found that wealth as well as wisdom can cast the shade needed to protect us from the sun's searing and potentially destructive rays—*under the shadow of wisdom, money too can provide shade* (7:12).

We then pondered the final phrase in that verse, *and the advantage of the knowledge of wisdom gives life to its owner,* and wrote as follows:

Given the combination of wisdom and possessions, there is integrity, there is balance and there is beauty. However, none of these suggest absolute equality. Wisdom may indeed be adorned by possessions, but it is no more than an adornment. Wisdom always retains dominance. It is ultimately the only one of the two that really matters.

Thus Koheles tells us that knowledge remains preeminent. It is only wisdom that grants a meaningful life (7:12).

These two verses can serve as the blueprint for Jewish life, for life well and Jewishly lived. They reflect precisely what we have said. In light of the fact that Succos celebrates our ordinary everyday lives lived within the embrace of the *succah's* sacred shade. And, in light of the fact that Shemini Atzeres insists that all of this alchemy can and must be brought into our solid, even seemingly autonomous homes, we learn that we would end up incomplete without the *advantage of the knowledge*, made explicit in our Simchas Torah.

*   *   *

We have called our thoughts on *Koheles, Give Seven Its Due*, because Koheles maintains that even the physical world, subsumed as it is under the concept "seven," has much to offer us in our service of God. Indeed, the megillah teaches us that within the confines of serving God with fear, an understanding of our physical world and its bounty is essential and, when handled well, salutary. But we have not yet paid sufficient attention to the "eight," the context of a higher sanctity which cradles this vision.

We turn to *Shabbos* 30b.

The Sages wanted to withdraw *Koheles* from circulation because some of its ideas seemed to contradict one another. Why did they decide otherwise? The book is redeemed by the fact that it both begins and ends with words of Torah. Torah animates the rhetorical question with which it begins: "What benefit is there for man in all his labors performed beneath the sun?" The implication is that futility lies only in a life lived under the sun. Inject Torah [that which was created before the sun (Rashi)] into the equation and life becomes very, very precious. Thus does the megillah begin with Torah.

It also ends with the celebration of Torah. The penultimate verse teaches: "The sum of the matter, when all has been considered: Fear God and keep His commandments for this is [what constitutes] man in his totality."

Rashi explains that the saving grace of the fact that *Koheles* both begins and ends with words of Torah is that, presented thus, we can be sure that Torah animates also all that is said in between.[4]

This, then, is the proposition which we are now called upon to consider. *Koheles* in its entirety is an expression of words of Torah. All of it, its denials and affirmations, its doubts and its conclusions, its hopes and its despairs, all, all of them are words of Torah. This, no doubt, includes all the positively lyric commendation of enthusiastic involvement in this-worldly activity, particularly as expressed in Chapter 11. But how can these affirmations be considered Torah, defined as it is as preceding the sun? It may be good, but it certainly is planted firmly in nature. It cannot be described as "before the sun."

It would appear that *Koheles* deals with three different modes of orientation which can be respectively described as 1. *Under the sun;* 2. *Before the sun;* and 3. That which animates people who *look upon the sun.* The megillah begins with an unqualified condemnation of life lived *under the sun.* The Gemara contrasts this kind of living to *before the sun,* which is its polar opposite and which parallels those virtues, awe and conscientious fulfillment of mitzvos, which the end of the megillah posits as the ideal human vocation. This coupling can be described as words of Torah, and it incorporates all that could be subsumed under that category.

The body of the megillah, to the extent that it views human endeavors positively (provided that they are performed by those who look upon the sun), would then be the expression of the middle ground. It can be described as words of Torah because the Torah endorses such activities, but of course they fall short of qualifying as before the sun.

It can now be said, and taking everything which we have

learned into account, it should be said, that the very positivism with which the megillah looks upon these activities is grounded in the fact that they are bracketed between the two passages which make the ascendancy of Torah in its capacity of *before the sun* paramount. It is as though the megillah were saying: Indeed, all this-worldly activities are worthy and are to be encouraged. But that is only true so long as it is understood that they fall short of the ideal. In the end *the advantage of knowledge* that is Torah counts for more. Only wisdom grants life to those who possess it.

And so Succos finds its inspiration in Simchas Torah.

There is no better way to end our little book than once more to borrow from the compositions of the poet for that glorious day:

אגיל ואשמח בשמחת תורה... תורה היא עץ חיים לכולם
חיים כי עמך מקור חיים

I will delight and rejoice in Simchas Torah…The Torah is a tree of life, life for all, because "with You is the source of life." (Machzor Simchas Torah)

ENDNOTES

1. Although we could quote almost any Rashi, we offer 8:10 as a particularly vivid example. It is an unusually difficult verse, and a glance at the standard commentators will show just how obscure its meaning really is. In spite of this, Rashi offers no exlanation at all and satisfies himself with a quote from the midrash:

ובכן ראיתי רשעים קבורים ובאו

And then I saw wicked ones who were buried but came,

וממקום קדוש יהלכו

who would go forward from a holy place,

וישתכחו בעיר אשר כן עשו

the deeds that they had done, forgotten in the city.

גם זה הבל

This too is futility.

Rashi comments that the "wicked ones who were buried" refers to gentiles who were considered so lowly among all the nations that it would really have been appropriate for them to have sunk into the earth, yet they nonetheless conquered the House of God, which is holy. And when they went away from there to their lands they boasted (*vayishtakchu,* to forget, is read homiletically as *vayishtabchu,* to praise) that this is what they had done to the Divine Temple. Thus is this verse interpreted in the Aggadah.

Now this entire rendering, which includes a reference to the destruction of the Temple which still lay four hundred years in the future, and including the homiletic substitution of one word with another, is entirely appropriate within the context of Aggadic thought. It is not, however, as Rashi makes very clear, the straightforward meaning of the verse.

We must therefore conclude that Rashi on this verse, as also on many others throughout Koheles, had an agenda other than the interpretation in accordance with the straightforward meaning.

2. For a discussion of this assertion see endnote #5 in the essay entitled *Shelter in the Shade*.

SHELTER IN THE SHADE

1. *Tehillim* 27:1 describes God as *Ori*, my light, and *Yishi*, my salvation. The midrash suggests that the quality of *ohr* is manifest on Rosh HaShanah, and the quality of *yesha* on Yom Kippur. On Yom Kippur, God saves us from our subordination to our evil instincts, our baser selves; on Yom Kippur, we become truly free. It is for this reason that many commentators see an affinity between the shofar that is sounded at the end of *Ne'ilah* with the one which ushers in the jubilee year. Both proclaim freedom throughout the land.

2. This analysis is based on *S'fas Emes*.

3. This derivation is reflected in the *halachah* that one of the absolute requirements for the *succah* to be kosher is that there be more shade than sun. If the *s'chach* were to be so sparsely applied that there would be a preponderance of sunlight, then it would not have any business to be defined as *s'chach*.

4. See *Yechezkel* 8:16 for a graphic picture of the idol worship which brought the first Temple to ruin: …*twenty-five men, their backs to the Temple of God, prostrating themselves before the sun.* (See the mishnah in *Succah* 51b for an account of how the memory of this dreadful event left its mark on the service during the second Temple.)

5. This thesis, that Succos celebrates the ordinary life lived extraordinarily within the confines of the *succah*, is perhaps the main theme that runs through most of the essays which comprise this book.

Some comments are in order.

The fact that we stress this particular aspect of the *succah* experience should not be taken as in any way limiting the enormous range of religious feelings and encounters which are an integral part of these awesome seven days. *Succah, Arba Minim, Hoshanos*, Simchas Beis HaSho'evah, all add their dimensions of breadth and depth. Even a cursory glance at the literature, particularly the genre of which the *Sfas Emes* could be viewed as representative, will yield an inkling of the wealth that is contained in each of these components of the holiday, both separately and together. Even within the mitzvah of *succah* which we have taken as our subject, there are layers upon layers of significance which go far beyond anything that we touch upon in these essays. We have taken one tiny jewel from the vast array spread out before us and have tried to polish it and define its contours so that it might fit comfortably into the setting which Koheles seems to provide for it.

Having said this, we should make a short digression into the mitzvah of the *Arba Minim*, in order to show that within that context too, there is a remarkable affinity to the idea which we have associated with that of the *succah*. There too, we come upon the concept of sublimating the apparently neutral into the sacred.

Vayikra 23:39 and 40 reads as follows:

But on the fifteenth day of the seventh month *when you gather in the crop of the land* you shall celebrate Hashem's festival for seven days.... You shall take for yourselves on the first day of the fruit of the citron tree, the branches of date palms, twigs of a plaited tree and brook willows and *you shall rejoice before Hashem your God for a seven day period.*

The context makes it clear enough. The four species are symbols of the crop which we have even now brought in, and they are to be used in helping us rejoice before God for the bounty which our fields have yielded. They are the appurtenances of a harvest festival, and that is all.

And yet that is not all at all. The midrashim are full of profound resonances: *pri eitz hadar* that is God; *kapos temarim* that is God; *anaf eitz avos* that is God; *ve'arvei nachal* that is God.... *Pri eitz hadar* that is Israel; *kapos temarim* that is Israel; *anaf eitz avos* that is Israel; *ve'arvei nachal* that is Israel, and on and on in a similar vein.

Taken in combination, the two midrashim which we have chosen clearly celebrate something very different than simply the bounties of a bumper harvest. We take our *Arba Minim* into our hands and we hold the secrets of Israel's history and destiny. We rejoice because these four species, each in its own way, whisper to us intimations of sanctity, of love, and of an identity with God's purpose which lifts us beyond the mundane and summons us to greatness.

Our attention is diverted from our bulging silos to our pulsating souls, from the riches of the field to the wealth within ourselves.

Our lulav and esrog have been transmuted from modest agricultural products into the weapons which signal the ultimate victory of good over evil, of Israel over its enemies (Midrash].

We have digressed into this discussion of the *Arba Minim* partly because a book of reflections on Succos would be incomplete without at least a brief and superficial analysis, but mainly to demonstrate that the theme of the *succah* which we have chosen to explore is reflected also in some of the other aspects of the holiday.

FINDING JOY IN UNLIKELY PLACES

1. The obligation to become inebriated on Purim to a point at which we can no longer distinguish between good and bad, can only be understood in such terms. So too the term *shagah*, to miss the mark, which Rambam favors in his discussion of *ahavah* in *Hilchos Teshuvah* ch. 10. This expression conveys the concept of a state of being in which the intellect is, at very best, quiescent.

2. The term *tachas hashemesh* occurs frequently in our megillah and we now turn our attention to the precise place which the sun occupies in aggadic literature.

   The sun, source of energy and life on earth, is the Torah's preeminent metaphor for the this-worldly and temporal.

   This is what Maharal has to say. We quote from Tif'eres 4: *For the sun controls nature, and all matter flourishes under its aegis. Because of this, … under the sun (Koheles 1:2) is the preferred metaphor when the physical world is to be described.*

   Accordingly, it stands to reason that when Koheles uses the expression *under the sun*, he is describing the world in it's "this-worldly", temporal sense. This frame of reference, as he demonstrates throughout the megillah, breeds only futility and stagnation.

3. Herewith is our analysis of the sources which yield our definition of *hevel*:

   Our quest takes us back to the very earliest beginnings of our history, into Noach's tent as he lies there in the sorry disgrace of his drunkenness. Cham has seen what he has seen, or done what he has done, and has told Shem and Yaphes what has happened. These two take a blanket, and with exquisite sensitivity enter backwards so as not to witness their father's shame, and cover his nakedness. However, all is not well with our text. In place of the expected plural form, *vayikchu*, and they took [the blanket], we have *vayikach*, in the singular. Our Sages explain this aberration. The initiative for this act of filial respect and loyalty came solely from Shem. He alone took the blanket initially. Yaphes allowed himself to be inveigled into this mission of mercy, but had no part in formulating it.

   For an understanding of the incident and an examination of its deeper meanings, we turn to Maharal (*Gur Aryeh* 9:23).

   In the tradition of the Sages, both Shem and Yaphes were rewarded for their sensitivity. Shem, from whom the Jewish people were to be descended, was given the mitzvah of tzitzis. Yaphes, precursor of the Gogian hordes which would one day fall in battle upon the hills of Israel, was granted that his slain descendants would be buried and not left to lie rotting upon the fields.

   The gifts were not arbitrarily chosen. They were designed to bestow honor upon those who had understood the concept of honor well enough to do what they had done. However, for Shem the initiator, the reward of the mitzvah of tzitzis addressed his soul; for Yaphes the follower, it was sufficient to honor the body and grant it the dignity of burial.

   This is so because active, vital initiation is the province of the soul, the life-force which energizes and animates us; while the passive plasticity of the follower is typified by the body, the eternal servant.

   Shem, projector of the vivifying life-force, is the one among Noach's three sons who parallels Adam's son Sheth, progenitor of all men and ultimately of Israel, the crown of humanity. Yaphes [from *yofi*, beauty, which is a function of the body] parallels Adam's son, Hevel [compare, *hevel hayofi* of Proverbs 31:30], the archetypal follower, the passive plastic personality which permits others to impress their initiatives upon it but is in itself non-creative and non-productive.

Our discovery of the Yaphes/Hevel pole can, claims Maharal, help us in our quest to obtain a true understanding of the term *vanity*. Adam's second son was given this name because it reflected the passivity of the body, which was his identifying feature as opposed to the animation of the soul. [Thus, for example, Cain discovers the revolutionary mode of divine service expressed in sacrifice; Hevel picks up the idea and improves upon it.]

We take our analysis further by examining the mitzvah of tzitzis, granted to the active Shem but denied the passive, plastic Yaphes.

We go to *Menachos* 43b where we learn of a certain man who had invested enormous expense and energy in pursuing a famous prostitute. When he had finally gained admittance and was about to approach her, his tzitzis came and slapped him in the face, preventing him, in the very last moment, from hopelessly compromising his standing as a Jew.

Maharal (*Chiddushei Aggadah*, to *Menachos*) explains as follows: Tzitzis (from *tzitz hasadeh*, that which grows out of the field) have the function of asserting the possibility of growth and expansion beyond that which might otherwise have been expected. There is no object that seems more absolutely limited than a square garment, bounded and defined by its four corners. Its grim boundaries seem to brook no defiance. Up to here and not beyond!

The tzitzis, threaded into the forbidding corners of the garment, mock this assertion. As little shoots, pushing their obstinate way up through the hard, harsh earth clods, announce to the world the irresistibility of their determined quest for life, so do the tzitzis, extending as they do beyond the confining edges of the garment, refuse to countenance the proposition that there are limits beyond which man simply cannot go. Boundaries hold no terrors for them. They flow on, unhindered and unbounded, into the far reaches of humanity's grasp.

The hero of the story in *Menachos* had thought that he was

no match for his desires. He saw no way at all in which he could maintain his religious integrity. His tzitzis came and slapped him on his face. "There is nothing," they were telling him, "that you cannot do. You are free, free to be yourself, free to say 'No!' when every feeling inside you screams that you must succumb to the urgings of your baser self."

This was the gift granted to Shem, the man of the soul, and denied Yaphes, the protagonist of the physical. Yaphes had beauty, *yofi*, but it was not the aesthetically delightful harmony of the fully controlled, fully disciplined, fully integrated moral personality, but the ephemeral beauty of appearance and form, bewitching to the eye but, in the final analysis, *vanity*.

We have come full turn and found a definition of the word *vanity* as perhaps the Maharal would understand it.

KOHELES AND THE STUDY OF THE TORAH

1. The word wisdom, of course, occurs many times. Rashi at 1:13 states unequivocally that this term is to be understood as Torah. However it seems unlikely that this would hold true at the *p'shat* level. The word wisdom, which we tend to associate with King Solomon, does not, in the first instance, seem to be Torah wisdom. The statement in *Melachim I* 5:10 and onwards, that his wisdom exceeded that of the Bnei Kedem and the Egyptians, that it enabled him to understand [or communicate with] the trees and animals and so on, and the statement there (verse 26) that it was King Solomon's wisdom that served as the basis for his friendship with Chirom—all these create the impression that some other form of wisdom is meant by the word wisdom.

    At the very outset of his reign, King Solomon asked for a *lev shomei'a*, a receptive heart, to help him in judging the people (*Melachim I* 3:9). God accepted his prayer and granted him a *lev chacham venavon*. We are then told of the two women who came before him, each claiming that her child was alive and that it was the child of the other woman who had died. King Solomon rendered his famous decision that the child was to be cut in half. This served to identify the true mother. This incident was seen by the people as evidence that *chachmas Elohim bekirbo la'asos mishpat*. Clearly this wisdom is a sophisticated insight into human nature [a "receptive heart" in the sense that experience with people was assimilated into an understanding of their nature] and not *chachmas haTorah* taken in its usual sense.

Even if we were to assume that *Koheles* is different and that there, in fact, the word always refers to Torah, we would still have to ask why wisdom, which has a much wider denotation than simply Torah (cf. *Midrash Eichah* 2:48 which contrasts wisdom, which can be found among the nations, with Torah, which cannot] is used exclusively, when Torah would seemingly have served as well. [To put this question in perspective we note that in *Mishlei*, both expressions are used, although admittedly wisdom preponderates.]

We shall consider Rashi's assertion, that the wisdom mentioned at 1:13 is Torah, in the more wide-ranging analysis of his ideas which forms the core of this essay.

2. It is noteworthy that in this verse King Solomon avoids any ambiguity. Torah, not wisdom, is used.

3. Our assertion that God loves the Torah is based on *Mishlei* 8:30 as explicated in many Midrashim, among them *Vayikra Rabba* 10:1.

4. Rashi's assumption that the *Isaiah* verse is to be taken metaphorically is, we assume, based on verse 3 there: *Hatu aznechem ulechu eilai*, Incline your ears and come to Me… which is taken as the explanation of the earlier verse. The exhortation to buy food is meant as an exhortation to open one's mind to the Torah's teaching.

5. The issue concerns the matter of carrying on Shabbos. For the purposes of the halachah, an ornament is not considered to be a "burden." If weapons are an ornament for the man who carries them, then if he takes them out on Shabbos he would not transgress the laws against carrying.

6. This interpretation of the rule that *ein mikra yotzei midei peshuto* is an almost verbatim translation of Ramban to *Sefer HaMitzvos Shoresh* 1 (p. 44 in the Chavel edition, Mosad HaRav Kook, Jerusalem 1981]. We quote:

כי אין הכונה להם אלא שיהיו הכתובים אמת במליצה ומשל ...

7. In fact, were it not for the Gemara's use of the phrase *ein mikra yotzei midei pshuto* in its description of the military theme, a use which certainly implies that the *Sage* theme is to be con-

trasted to *pshuto* and considered *derash*, we would not have used the terms *p'shat* and *derash* at all. The *"p'shat"* of a metaphor [understood as the sole message that is to be conveyed] is certainly that for which the metaphor stands and not the bare-bones words that are being used. These would better be called *"mishma"* as in the phrase *pshuto kemishma'o*, the meaning of which seems to be that the *p'shat*, that is the message, is, in that particular case, congruent with the *mishma*, the plain meaning of the words. Clearly the Gemara is using *"p'shat"* [and by inference *"derash"*] broadly.

8. We have confined ourselves to translating the words as they stand. Clearly such a reference to Yitzchak Avinu cannot be taken at face value. However, in the context of our analysis of the relationship between *p'shat* and *derash*, the discovery and discussion of the deeper meaning of such a statement have no place.

9. The context of our discussion is too narrow to allow for a complete analysis of this passage. However, we should note in passing that it is not easy to see why the one interpretation is claimed as *p'shat* and the other as *derash*. It is a fact that the words as they stand yield the *derash* more readily than they do the *p'shat*. For the *p'shat* meaning we have to add some words (see, for example, Ibn Ezra and Ramban's remarks] while the *derash* interpretation fits smoothly into the text as it appears.

   A careful consideration of these and related issues appears in a German essay by the late Dr. Eduard Biberfeld in vol. 7 of the *Jahrbuch der Jüdisch—Literarischen Geselschaft* 1909.

10. We assume that the *p'shat* reading which legitimizes the enjoyment of life's simple pleasures would be applicable to the general populace for whom the Shulchan Aruch (*Orech Chaim* 155 and 156] counsels a judicious mix of serious Torah study and pursuit of a decent livelihood. For such people—the "many" who follow Rabbi Yishmael's advice that Torah is to be accompanied by Derech Eretz (*Berachos* 35b)—"eating" and "drinking," that is the whole exercise of leading a wholesome and balanced existence, is a significant component of a life well lived. It is for such as these that Rambam sets forth his detailed regimen for healthy eating (*De'os* 3:2 and elsewhere), healthy sleeping (*De'os* 4:4) and prudent management of one's financial resources (*De'os* 5:11–12).

The *derash* would be relevant to the "individuals who are to be found in every generation" (Be'ur Halachah *Orech Chaim* 156) who have emancipated themselves from all these mundane considerations and for whom only Torah has any real meaning. (See Endnote #1 to the essay entitled *Labor*). These are the ones who fight the body's craving for sleep and who will eat only the barest minimum to keep life and energy going (*Talmud Torah* 3:12). They are our royalty—those who have wrested the Keser HaTorah, the Torah's crown, from the cloying chains of ordinariness (*Talmud Torah* 3:13).

It seems particularly apt that King Solomon's thoughts for the masses are couched in the *p'shat* of the megillah while those for the elite find expression in the *derash*. As we have demonstrated (see Endone #12), *p'shat* relates to *derash* as does surface to depth, the more superficial to the more profound. It is only those chosen few who will search [*doresh*] diligently who will find the *derash* beneath the *p'shat*, the true essence beneath the form.

The Rebbi of my youth, HaRav Aryeh Carmel, to whom I also owe the insights into the Rambam which I have adumbrated above, believes that these two equally legitimate ways of serving God are expressed in the two interpretations offered in Temurah 16a for Yaavetz's prayer:

With fertility	*With Torah*	אם ברך תברכני
With sons and daughters	*With students*	והרבית את גבולי
In business	*That I remember my learning*	והיתה ידך עמי
That I maintain good health	*That I find peers who are congenial to me*	ועשית מרעה
That my evil inclination not prevent me from learning	*That my evil inclination not prevent me from learning*	לבלתי עצבי

We have an almost eerie feeling of two discrete worlds which think different thoughts, subscribe to different values and talk in languages which the other cannot understand. The significant truth for our purposes is that both are petitions offered seriously and humbly before God and that both were answered by a God who understands and values the honest aspirations of every heart.

11. My choice of *Teshuvas R' Akiva Eiger* as an example derives from personal experience. As a youngster, I attended a shiur given by a venerable Yiddish speaking Sage who was trying, without too much success, to make a group of us young Americans follow the intricacies of his exposition of one of these highly complex *teshuvos*. Suddenly he interrupted his presentation and broke into a sweet smile. With almost child-like enthusiasm he tried to inveigle us into the magic web of his burning love. As good as smacking his lips, he burst out:

קינדערלך, תורה איז דאך א מאכל, ס'איז ממש אן אמת"ע מאכל!

If you know Yiddish, you will be able to imagine this scene. The phrase is untranslatable.

12. It is in this thickening relationship between *p'shat* and *derash* that the real meaning of these two expressions is best projected. *P'shat* derives from the root *poshat*, to spread out, and denotes the interpretation of the words which is open and obvious to all. *Derash* derives from the root, *dorash*, to seek out, and denotes a reading which digs beneath the surface in order to find hidden, hitherto unsuspected implications.

13. For an expansion on this theme, see Endnote #2 to the next essay. Note the reference there to *Chullin* 6b where the Gemara asserts that the *p'shat* meaning of *Mishlei* 23:1–2 which talks of eating in the presence of a ruler, deals with the study of Torah; the ruler mentioned in the verse to be taken as a Torah teacher. Nevertheless, Rashi, in his commentary to *Mishlei*, has the verse deal with an actual meal taken in the presence of an actual ruler.

    This is a precise example of what we have here. Both are the "true" meaning of the verse. Different ears will pick up different nuances.

14. Some examples are 1:13, 2:3 and 2:12.

15. This conclusion cannot be absolutely affirmed. We cannot ignore the possibility that the word wisdom must simply be defined by context. Occasionally it will mean general wisdom, occasionally Torah. The reader or commentator must simply use his intuition or judgment to read the meaning correctly.

The fact that different readings are possible need of course not be labored. The issue at hand is no different than the myriad problems with which commentators grapple and solve according to their own predilections. Nevertheless we will bring just an example from the three sources cited in the previous Endnote to illustrate. Metzudos at 2:3 interprets wisdom as does Rashi to mean Torah, but at 1:13 and 2:12 he reads the word more broadly.

LIVING LIFE TO THE FULLEST

16. Rashi interprets the passage as an exhortation to be satisfied and even happy with that which he earns by the labor of his hands and not to crave wealth which was not apportioned to him. See also Rashi at 5:17.

17. As we shall see within, this passage appears to be much more radical than any of the others. It seems to advocate an appreciation of the simple joys of life even for someone who is still functioning "under the sun."

At first blush, this assertion seems to fly in the face of the ideas which we impute to Koheles throughout these essays. His thesis, as we understand it, is that physical life can indeed be beautiful and positive as long as it can escape the "under the sun" orientation which he constantly and consistently bemoans as *vanity*.

But that he should countenance pleasure in life lived "under the sun" seems out of character with everything else that the megillah seems to assert.

Perhaps we are to conclude that Koheles's affirmation of a positive value to ordinary living experiences is so strong that he would recommend it even for those who, for lack of energy to change their orientation, are still living "under the sun." Negativism will never get anybody anywhere.

There is another possibility which could legitimately be explored.

Our verse appears between the only two verses in Koheles which use *al ha'aretz* as a synonym for *under the sun* or *tachas hashamayim*. We have discussed these terms in detail in *Making do*. A close reading of verses 14–17 yields that, at least in this passage, *under the sun* is used interchangeably with *al ha'aretz*.

The explanation might be as follows:

The entire thrust of this passage is to decry the impossibility of ever understanding the way things happen in our world. Koheles is shattered by the seeming injustice of so much that he observes. The righteous suffer, the wicked prosper, and everything that we do or leave undone seems to make no difference at all. Life seems to be an exercise in futility.

In this context, the constant interchanging of the terms *al ha'aretz* and *under the sun* is an enormously powerful literary tool. It conveys the sense of despair that envelops Koheles when he sees that what happens "*al ha'aretz*," in the normal course of events as we defined this term in *Making Do*, seems precisely what we would expect if the world were truly "*under the sun.*"

If the whole passage is read in this way, it transpires that the use of *under the sun* in these few verses has a different connotation than in the rest of the megillah. It is a description of how things appear in our moments of despair.

18. A word is in place concerning Rashi's commentary to these passages. The issue is a particularly important one and we will treat it in greater detail than would normally be appropriate for this series of essays. We have numbered the passages within, and shall follow these same numbers in this endnote:

Rashi	Text
... והראה את נפשו טוב כלומר **יתן לבו לעשות משפט וצדקה עם** המאכל והמשתה	1. אין טוב באדם שיאכל ושתה **והראה את נפשו טוב** בעמלו גם זה ראיתי אני כי מיד האל־הים היא. (2:24)
וראה טוב: **תורה ומצוות.**	2. וגם כל האדם שיאכל ושתה **וראה טוב** בכל עמלו מתת אל־הים היא. (3:13)
מאשר ישמח במעשיו: **ביגיע כפיו** וישמח ויאכל ...	3. וראיתי כי אין טוב מאשר ישמח האדם **במעשיו** כי הוא חלקו ... (3:22)
והשליטו לאכל ממנו: **בחייו ... לעסוק בתורה ובמצוות** בחייו ...	4. גם כל האדם אשר נתן לו האל־הים עשר ונכסים **והשליטו לאכל ממנו ולשאת** את חלקו ולשמח בעמלו זה מתת אל־הים היא. (5:18)
לאכל ולשתות: ממה שנתן לו הקב"ה ולשמח בחלקו. ומדרש אגדה: **כל אכילה ושתיה שבקוהלת אינה אלא תלמוד תורה ...**	5. ושבחתי אני את השמחה אשר אין טוב לאדם תחת השמש כי אם **לאכל ולשתות** ולשמוח ... (8:15)
... אתה הצדיק שכבר רצה הקב"ה מעשיך הטובים ... **לך אכל בשמחה ...**	6. **לך אכל בשמחה** לחמך ושתה בלב טוב יינך ... (9:7)

Our chart, by setting the words that are being interpreted and the interpretation which Rashi offers in bold, illustrates clearly that at the *p'shat* level *achilah* and *shesiyah* are to be taken at face value. This is precisely as we have done within, and only at the level of mi*drash* are they to be taken as Torah study.

To make this important difference absolutely clear, we need to go a little further afield. Our focus will be on *Mishlei* 23:1–2 as these verses are discussed in *Chullin* 6b:

כי תשב ללחום את מושל בין תבין את אשר לפניך ושמת סכין
בלועיך אם בעל נפש אתה

When you sit down to dine with a ruler, know well what lies before you, and put a knife to your throat if you are a master of [your] soul.

After the Gemara had made use of the verse in a way which patently did not accord with its simple meaning, it poses the question:

פשטיה דקרא במאי כתיב

What, in fact, does the verse really convey to us?

The Gemara answers that it refers to a student sitting in front of his master. The words, "When you sit down to dine with a ruler…" are to be taken metaphorically. Eating is a metaphor for learning, and so on.

Now the wording which the Gemara uses: *pashta d'kra bemai ksiv*, would seem to imply that interest is focused on the actual simple [*p'shat*] meaning of the verse. The answer would then have to be understood as asserting that the metaphorical usage is in fact the simple meaning of the words. This would have to be based on the assumption that the ordinary etiquette of eating with princes would not be of interest to Holy Scripture.

If this is indeed the meaning of the Gemara, it would then put our earlier assertion concerning the *Koheles* passages into question. We asserted that there is a world of *p'shat* in which *Koheles* recommends taking simple joy in simple pleasures, and a world of *derash* in which eating and drinking stand for the study of Torah. However, in light of the above, perhaps the *p'shat* world does not exist at all. *Koheles* is as unlikely to be concerned about physical eating and drinking as is *Mishlei*. Perhaps all these passages must, even at the *p'shat* level, be considered metaphorical.

However, such a conclusion is not warranted. A careful analysis of the meaning of the phrase *pashta d'kra bemai ksiv*, as it is used in most places throughout Shas, demonstrates that it is not the *"p'shat"* level of meaning which is at the center of the Gemara's concern. Rather, as in the case of the *Chullin* passage, the question usually follows an instance where a particular verse was used as a hint to some issue which could not possibly be fitted into the context of which the verse is a part. When that is done, the Gemara will then ask *pashta d'kra bemai ksiv* in order to ascertain the real meaning of the verse in the context in which it occurs. That meaning, however, may well be at the *derash* level rather than that of *p'shat*. The *"pashta"* does not mean *"p'shat"* as opposed to *"derash,"* but context oriented *derash* as opposed to non-context oriented *derash.*

If confirmation for this assertion is required, we find it in Rashi's commentary to *Mishlei.* Here he takes the verse as guiding us in the way we should dine with a ruler, rather than in the sense which *Chullin* describes as *pashta.*

19. Our formulation throughout this passage seems rather bland. We talk of enjoying life's simple pleasures as though that were all there is to our interaction with the physical world of which we are a part. Certainly, great Jewish thinkers throughout the ages, whether they couched their ideas in the language of philosophy, Mussar or Torah Im Derech Eretz, have had much to say about more profound and meaningful ways of dealing with the this-worldly.

We must remember that *Koheles* does not exist in a vacuum, but that it is part of TaNaCH which, together with all the relevant comments of the Sages, must be taken in its totality if we are to garner a comprehensive and authentically Jewish world view. In our small essay, we are not attempting to present anything beyond that which the text of *Koheles* says, taken at its simplest level. This is nothing more than the raw material from which the Talmidei Chachamim of every generation and in all their variegated thought-worlds fashioned and continue to fashion the rich Judaism which is our life.

20. Thus the midrash. The count is based on the uses of *vanity* in both its singular and plural forms. There are three singular uses, making three, and two plurals which count as two each. Thus we have a total of seven.

21. We are taking the concept further than the Gemara seems to warrant. The expression which the Gemara uses is:

... תחת השמש הוא דאין לו קודם השמש יש לו

To which Rashi remarks:

קודם השמש: אם יעמול בתורה שקדמה לשמש יש יתרון

Ostensibly, then, the only *amal* which is worthwhile would be the study of Torah.

However, what is significant for our purposes is that the Gemara limits the opprobrium expressed in 1:3 to such *amal* as is undertaken *under the sun.* Between that and the *amal* of

Torah which is described as *kodem hashemesh*, there is obviously some middle ground. It is upon this neutral ground that our thoughts are focused.

22. Compare:

מה יתרון לאדם בכל עמלו שיעמול תחת השמש

23. See Endnote #1 in the essay entitled *Labor*.

24. We need not belabor the point that for Hillel himself, even the negative formulation which he used would assume obligations and ideas of which no secular humanist could ever dream. But even with this granted, there is no reason to suppose that the gentile who came to him would be privy to those subtleties. He heard the words which Hillel used and understood them at their face value as any man in his position would. Hence the problem with which we are grappling.

PROBLEMS

1. The expression, *malei lev,* is very unusual. It recurs only at *Esther 7:5, asher mela'o libo....* We are, of course, dealing with an idiom which ought not to be taken literally. Nevertheless, since *malei* means to be full, we are probably justified in assuming that the sense of the expression is to describe someone who is so focused on one particular assumption that it fills his entire mind and leaves no room for seeing more than one side to the question.

   If the people who are being described here would leave room in their minds for other possible explanations of the seeming injustice—that is, delayed justice—which they are witnessing, the odds are that they might avoid being seduced into drifting into a life of evil.

   It is worthwhile to spend a few moments to learn Koheles's recommendations for avoiding the dead-end of fossilized assumptions.

ביום טובה היה בטוב

וביום רעה ראה

גם את זה לעמת זה עשה האל־הים

על דברת שלא ימצא האדם אחריו מאומה (7:14)

   This is not an easy verse to translate. We will render it as literally as possible while recognizing that some of the expressions are idiomatic. Armed with the basic translation, we will see whether we can penetrate the abstruse language and get to the heart of the sentiment that is being expressed.

On good days, be a part of that goodness.

But on bad days—just watch.

The two have congruent characteristics—both are brought about by God.

Thus that man cannot in the least understand His motives.

The key to the understanding of the first two stitches surely lies in the contrast between *heyai betov* and *re'ai*. Both are exhortations. The former tells us what we are to be [*heyai*], the latter what we are to do [*re'ai*]. Now in *Shadows*, we establish that *re'ai* is used by Koheles to describe an independent stance from which it is possible to observe objectively without being shackled by subjective involvement [*lir'os es hashemesh* in contrast to *under the sun*]. Accordingly, the meaning is clear: When things are going well, when everyone is happy, when doubts and fears do not becloud the horizon, then *heyai betov*. We are to be a part of the joy, allow it to engulf us, to define us and to change us. However, when things go badly, then *re'ai*. We are to retain our objective perspective, and not to permit ourselves to be dragged down into a morass of dejection. We are to observe what is happening, ponder its implications, try to understand it and thus allow the balm of wisdom to heal our pain.

The verse then goes on to explain that even bad times, since these also come from God, can yield positive lessons. Why He should want to do so is beyond human ken, but clearly He determined that there be a balance between the two forces of good and evil.

This then is the advice which Koheles proffers. When faced with seemingly insoluble problems, we are to stand back and consider what we can learn from them rather than allowing ourselves to be overwhelmed by the sheer inexplicability of the sway which evil can and does wield over our lives.

2. In fact, we cannot exclude the possibility that the verse ought to be translated differently than we have taken it. Perhaps we are not dealing with a question and an answer, but with one cohesive statement. Perhaps the sentence should be translated: The

fact that the sinner does what is wrong for a hundred… makes me realize that it will be well with those who fear God….

However, while this is an appealing translation if the sentence were to be standing on its own, it does not fit comfortably in to the context of the whole section.

3. For the justification for this translation, see Ramban, *Bereishis* 25:28, who demonstrates that in Hebrew usage a person can be described as the personification of a quality with which he is particularly identified. Thus David sings *ani tefillah*, I am [the embodiment of] prayer. Or, *ani shalom*, I am [the embodiment of] peace.

MAKING DO

4. The precise meaning of *under the sun* has been covered in *Finding Joy in Unlikely Places*. For *tachas hashamayim* we present our thoughts here:

At 5:1 we read:

... ולבך אל ימהר להוציא דבר לפני האל·הים כי האל·הים
בשמים ואתה על הארץ על כן יהיו דבריך מעטים

… let your heart not be too quick to utter words before God because God is in heaven and you are on the earth, therefore let your words be few.

How are we to understand the reasoning? The answer may well lie in Maharal's explanation of the term *mora shamayim*, fear of Heaven, which is commonly used where we would have expected *mora Hashem*, fear of God, much as we talk of *ahavas Hashem* and not *ahavas shamayim*.

Maharal's solution is that the term *mora shamayim* is particularly apt for expressing the awe which is the essence of *yir'ah*. That sense of awe derives from an awareness of distance. I stand in awe of that which must forever be beyond my ken, the One Whose otherness is absolute. The term *shamayim* conveys just this sense of distance. [Compare Hirsch's explanation of the word *shamayim*, the double *shom*, there, the absolute and unbridgeable "thereness."] In this, the *avodas hayir'ah* is the direct opposite of *avodah me'ahavah*. Love draws its energy from a sense of togetherness, a oneness which knows no barriers. *Ahavas shamayim*, the love of a distant, unattainable object, would be a contradiction in terms. Accordingly, we speak only of *ahavas Hashem*. But *yir'ah* is different. It is a mode of relating to the beyond, a set of attitudes based upon the realization of such profound separation that it would never be able to tolerate the use of God's name. Nothing but *mora shamayim* will do.

Accordingly, we suggest that whenever the megillah uses *tachas hashamayim* rather than *under the sun*, the passage is to be interpreted in a positive sense. It signals a discussion of what the *avodah miyir'ah* might demand in a given set of conditions.

5.   The usage is reminiscent of *kol ha'adam*, an expression which Koheles uses on a number of occasions. We have discussed the meaning of this phrase in *Living Life to the Fullest*.

6.   It seems boundlessly significant that we have here a *kri/ksiv*, that the word is written one way but pronounced another. It is well attested that in many instances where this is the case, the *ksiv*, the written form, is, as it were, the soul, the energizing force of the *kri*, the spoken form.

Here we read *yechubar* [from *chavar*, to join], to be joined, but the word is written, *yivchar* [from *bachar*, to choose], he will make choices. The implication is that it is necessary to be in a position to make choices if one is to be connected to life as it should be lived.

PRISMS

7.   I have tried my best with a difficult verse. The Hebrew reads:

אשר עשה האל־הים את האדם ישר והמה בקשו חשבונות רבים

The English word "straight" conveys very little of the highly nuanced *yashar*. I have seen translations which use "simple" or "plain," but neither ring true. In such a situation, an honest translation must resort to paraphrase.

8.   Once more I have had to settle for a paraphrase of the sentence.

Herewith my justification:

1.   *Mi kehachacham*: This is an exclamation of admiration for the wise man. A literal rendition would have made it sound more like a question.

2.   *Umi yodei'a peisher davar*: Given the correct understanding of the first phrase, the "else" follows logically.

For our rendition of *peisher davar*, see within. We have tried to make room for both possible meanings of *peisher.*

3. and 4. are more or less self-explanatory. For further elucidation see within.

9. We have the word *poshrin* for lukewarm water. This usage clearly derives from the meaning of compromise which the root carries. It is, as it were, a compromise between hot and cold.

10. We understand the rest of the verse as follows:

An inner light suffuses the face of the wise man. None of the bitter disillusionment of the frustrated, fragmented victim here. None of the darkness that is the hallmark of the habitual loser.

And there is strength. Strength because there is control. There is the calm confidence of one who has his tools at hand and knows how to make them do what he wants. People recognize competence. If you have it, you stand out.

We have rendered *yeshuneh* as, *he stands out.* Well and good. *Shanah* is the word denoting difference. But why should the word be spelled with the Aramaic *alef*? Why *yeshuneh* with an *alef* rather than the Hebrew *yeshuneh* with a *heh*?

[A word is in order concerning our contention that the root word *shin, nun, alef* is an Aramaism rather than a Hebrew verb form such as *tzaddi, mem, alef.*

Throughout those books which are written in Aramaic, *shin, nun, alef* is used exclusively. In the Hebrew books it is always *shin, nun, heh* except in our verse, *Eichah* 4:1, and *Melachim* II 25:29.

Of these, the *Melachim* passage is of particular interest because it parallels *Yirmiyah* 52:33 where the expected *shin, nun, heh* is used.

Clearly, then, *shin, nun, alef* is an alternative spelling to *shin, nun, heh* rather than an independent verb form. Accordingly, in each case we need to examine why it was used. In the present context it is the *Koheles* verse which commands our attention.]

Being strong is one thing, being loved is another. It seems quite possible that Koheles is telling us that behind every *yeshuneh* [with a *heh*] lurks a *yesuneh* [with an *alef*, from *sin, nun, alef*, to hate]. Behind everyone who dares to be different, to draw conclusions and to follow them wherever they might lead, there are the timid and the vacillating who dare not probe beneath the surface simplicities and who resent those who do. The *az panim* is not only different [*yeshuneh* with a *heh*], but he is also roundly disliked [*yesuneh* with an *alef*] for his troubles.

11. We have translated this passage loosely, based on the German rendering of the late Rabbi Joseph Carlebach *Hy"d*.

12. A word is warranted concerning our rendering of *ba'alei asuphos*. Rashi, in maintaining that the term describes a certain type of nail, is not followed by any of the major commentators, and certainly does not accord with the Midrashic interpretation of the expression.

Broadly speaking, we have two diverse approaches. The Midrashim take *asufah* as a gathering and assume that Koheles refers to the Sages when they get together in groups to discuss ideas which, while they may cover a wide range of perceptions, nevertheless all emanate from one God. The commentators prefer to read the term as describing what the wise do. They gather their knowledge from many written sources.

We have rendered the term in accordance with the latter meaning but have expanded it to include experience as well as books. The sages are as wise as they are, precisely because they have used all of life's vicissitudes to enrich their understanding and to confirm their belief that ultimately all that life has to offer is an expression of God's will.

MAN AND MAN

1. At creation, the entire world was filled with vegetable and animal life. Millions of trees, millions of mosquitoes. By contrast, Adam HaRishon was created singly. There was no other person besides him.

2. The immediate sense of this teaching is, of course, not as I have used it here. Rashi comments: [Man is to derive from the fact that he was created singly that] inasmuch as my existence is sufficiently significant to have an entire cosmos created just for me, it would be foolish to lose all this just for the pleasure which one sin might give me. If he thinks along these lines, it will help him not to sin.

However, it seems obvious that this intellectual conclusion

would not be possible if it were not confirmed by a strong instinctive feeling that, indeed, I and no other am at the center of things.

MAN AND WOMAN

3. Rashi notes as follws:

> Koheles is a feminine form. When [as in the rest of the megillah] it is treated as masculine it refers to the person, Shlomo, who does the gathering [see Rashi to 1:1 that the protagonist is called Koheles, *al shem shekiheil chachmos harbeh*, because he gathered together much wisdom]. When used in the feminine form it refers the wisdom itself which was gathered, or to the soul [*nefesh* is a feminine word], the *nefesh hamaskeles* which was responsible for the gathering.

Rashi has explained the usage but gives no indication why just here, and nowhere else in the megillah, the *gathered* wisdom or the *nefesh hamaskeles* rather the person himself, is invoked.

Perhaps this change from surface to sub-surface consciousness can be explained on the basis of the thesis which we suggested in the text and upon which we expand in the next Endnote. We are dealing with reflections which were inspired in a moment of personal weakness or failing. Such thoughts would not break through completely to the level of consciousness. They are intuited rather than expressed.

Thus, our thoughts tie in well with Rashi's explanation of the unique form in which this verse is couched.

4. Our statement that King Solomon said what he said in a moment of personal weakness needs some clarification. We do not normally make such judgments about the great and holy figures who people our TaNaCH. It is therefore important to place this assertion into a proper context. We will try to do this in one of two ways. The first addressing the particular issue at hand and the second attempting a wider sweep.

In a remarkable passage, *BaMidbar Rabba* 10:4, Bas Sheva, King Solomon's mother, criticizes him for allowing feminine influence, inappropriately, to affect his behavior. She rebuked him with the words from *Mishlei* 31:2: *Al titein lanashim cheilecha...*, Do not subordinate your power to women.

Here is the background to the story. Tradition has it that

King Solomon married Pharaoh's daughter on the very day that the Temple was inaugurated. The two celebrations were held concurrently and the wedding celebration was the more elaborate of the two. An analysis of this matter lies beyond the purview of this short essay but it is important to note the Midrash's assertion that it was at that moment that the seeds of the ultimate destruction of the Temple were sown.

The next morning Shlomo overslept. Pharaoh's daughter had planned it that way, and she accomplished exactly what she had wanted. The people were devastated. This was the day which they had anticipated for so long and there they were, standing in the Temple Courtyard, unable to move ahead without the king. Nobody had the courage to wake him. In desperation they turned to Bas Sheva for help.

The Midrash describes what happened:

She went and woke him up, strapped him to a [whipping] pole and berated him: "Everybody knows that your father David was a God-fearing man [and he will not be blamed for this disgrace]. People will say that it is I, your mother, who is to be faulted...

"Do not subordinate your power to women! ...Excessive pursuit of sexual gratification addles the mind..."

It seems to me that King Solomon may well have experienced such a moment as one of inner weakness. It is likely that he knew or at least intuited that he had inadvertently, but nevertheless through his own weakness, guaranteed the destruction of the very edifice which he had only now inaugurated with so much love. He might well have decried the feminine weakness within himself which had allowed the Bas Pharaoh to manipulate him. He must have seen now that marrying her was a terrible mistake.

So much for the case at hand.

There is also the following consideration.

Our tradition is unequivocal that the Book of *Koheles* was written by King Solomon. It is however nowhere stated whether the protagonist, Koheles, is meant to be King Solomon himself or whether he is an imaginary person through whom Shlomo is able to reach us and teach us.

There are several cogent arguments for the second possibility. In the first place, there is nothing in *Koheles* which makes open reference to any of the events which are known to us from *Melachim* and *Divrei HaYamim*. If here and there midrashim or some commentators do read a passage as referring to a known event, there are always others who have a different interpretation. Certainly there is nothing at all that is explicit.

There is also the matter of the first two chapters of the book in which Koheles describes the various experiments which he made along the road of his quest to find the ideal mixture of wisdom and folly in a life well lived. Some of these—particularly those which toy with the idea of a complete rejection of wisdom as an operative force—seem strange indeed if Koheles is to be identified with King Solomon. He, after all, at the very beginning of his kingship, when he was still a child, wanted nothing other than wisdom to guide him along the path to which destiny had directed him.

It is much more likely that Koheles is an imaginary king whom King Solomon uses as a protagonist through whose cogitations and uncertainties he reaches the all-important message of his book—that at the end of the day, the only thing that really matters is a life lived in fear of God and in the conscientious fulfillment of His mitzvos.

Accordingly, we need not, in discussing Koheles the man, face the same inhibitions which would limit us in talking of King Solomon. Koheles's life and thought, not that of King Solomon, chart the path from weakness to strength, from doubt to self-assurance, from physicality to spirituality, which we have seen again and again are at the core of the megillah's celebration of emancipation from life lived *under the sun.*

MAN AND WIFE

5. Our own benighted generation, in which all standards have been jettisoned and in which society with lemming-like determination seems bent upon self-destruction, may be an exception.

6. Some examples chosen at random are: In the presence of…, *Shemos* 34:10; Opposite, *Shemos* 19:2; Over against, *Bereishis* 21:16; Towards, *Tehillim* 31:20.

7. See *Man and Woman* for the relationship between the words *ish* and *ishah*.

8. The assumption here is that *adam*, man, is related to *adamah*, earth.

9. *Bereishis* 2:23 is the first time that Adam is referred to as *ish*. Before that verse, he was known only at *adam* (Yitzchak Breuer).

10. *Mishlei* 18:22. *Matza ishah matza tov* lends itself to two possible translations. It could, of course, mean that he who has found a wife has found goodness [that is, because marriage is good], but it could also mean that he has discovered the good that was latent in himself. Through his wife's loving eyes, he discovers aspects of his personality which he himself had never before recognized.

11. In his sermon on *Koheles*, Ramban finds common ground between *hevel* as futility and *hevel* as breath as in *hevel tinokos shel beis rabban*. He connects the two by noting how insubstantial is the breath which is visible on a cold day. It is there for a second and then it disappears. Such is the *vanity* of which Koheles talks.

    In the context of our thinking, we might suggest a different relationship. A person who breathes out is projecting only that which comes from within himself. There is nothing at all of another in that which issues forth from his mouth. That single-minded concentration on the self is the true essence of futility. Creative and productive living can only come about when others are drawn into the ambit of our concerns.

WEALTH

1. And this, in spite of King Solomon's plea, *raysh va'osher al titein li*, that God give him neither excessive poverty nor excessive wealth (*Mishlei* 30:8).

    There is really no contradiction. King Solomon does not deny that he craves wealth as does everyone else. He is just terrified of what might happen if he actually becomes rich. *Pen esba vechichashti ve'amarti mi Hashem*, Lest I become satiated and will then disavow [God], will proclaim, "Who is Hashem." He knows the arrogance that is the dark side of power, knows the inability of those wallowing in luxury to look beyond themselves.

And he is afraid.

He might well have prayed for wealth—and still prayed that God not answer his prayer.

This ambivalence is expressed by the prayer which we say on the Shabbos before Rosh Chodesh, following immediately upon asking for *osher vechavod*. We pray that our lives might be filled with the fear of heaven *veyir'as cheit*, fear of God and fear of sin. We have our doubts about the degree to which we can trust ourselves. We need all the help which we can get.

2. We should note that Rashi has a different interpretation to this verse. We discuss this Rashi together with many similar ones in *Living Life to the Fullest*.

LABOR

3. It is worth nothing Beur Halachah's remarks:

> It has been noted that this halachah applies only to the general populace, not all of whom are able to attain the lofty levels of piety which would make it possible for them to devote their entire lives to Torah. But certainly each generation will have its individuals who are well able to center their entire lives upon the study of Torah.

Chovos HaLevavos in *Shaar HaBitachon* feels that God's purpose in demanding that we take responsibility for making a living was twofold: If there were no need to go to work in order to feed, clothe and shelter our families, many people would be hard put to fill their days usefully. With nothing much to do, boredom would drive them to sin and destructive behavior. Moreover, the marketplace with all its drives and passions can and does test the mettle of our commitment to the Torah values of honesty, integrity, trust in God and so on. It is for these two reasons that God placed the burden of providing ourselves with a living upon our shoulders.

Accordingly, Chovos HaLevavos reasons that anyone who has already proved himself on these two fronts would be relieved from this obligation. If he has shown that he will use his time constructively, if his dealings in all areas are so obviously in accordance with the standards which the Torah wants from us that no more corroboration could be required, then he has the right to devote his entire life to learning and put his trust in God who will provide him with his needs.

4. See Maharal, *Ner Mitzvah*, p.28. The poem at the end of the haggadah, *az rov nissim hifleisa ba'laylah*, bears out our contention. Miracles tend to take place at night.

5. Our rendering of Adam as striver requires some clarification.

In the course of these essays, we have attempted, where appropriate, to offer in-depth definitions of some of the key words which lend body and nuance to *Koheles*. *Adam* is one of the words which occurs with sufficient frequency to require careful analysis.

We turn to Maharal in *Tiferes* 3. He questions why man among all living creatures should be called *adam* which derives from *adamah*, earth. According to the Torah's account of the creation, the entire animal world was brought forth from the earth [... *totzei ha'aretz nefesh chayah*] and thus any or all of its denizens could apparently with equal validity have been called *Adam*.

Clearly, then, it is not because man was created from the earth that he is called *Adam*. Rather, it is because he, and only he, shares one of earth's salient features. A clod of earth has very little intrinsic value. Nevertheless, it carries within itself the potential for all life. All sentient beings must ultimately turn to it for their sustenance. It may be defined as that which has value only in that which it can produce, never in that which it is within itself.

That, too, is the nature of man. His value is never in what he is; only in what he can become. God's seal of approval, the *Vayar ... ki tov* which throughout the creation narrative testifies to the absolute value of all that He brought into being, is absent from the account of Adam's creation. God's "seeing that it was good" is the expression of His will that the given unit ought indeed to be as it is (Ramban, *Bereishis* 1:4). Manifestly, that is not the case with man. As long as there is another second of life within him, he is not yet as he ought to be. There is still work to be done, there are heights to be scaled, worlds to be conquered.

In accordance with this analysis, we have identified Adam as the striver.

6. See Hirsch on *Bereishis* 3:20 in his explanation of why the woman was called *Chavah* related to *yechaveh da'as* rather than *Chayah*, the life-force.

7. The difference (see Tosafos, *Bava Kama* 38a s.v. *ela ha'adam*) is that the word *adam* can refer only to a Jew, while *ha'adam* describes every human being. Tiferes Yisrael (*Avos* 3:1 Boaz) explains as follows: When the Torah uses *Adam* it is meant as a proper noun, the given name of the first man. Only Yisrael, Adam's spiritual heir, can lay claim to that name. *Ha'adam* simply means man—one of the properties of a proper noun is that it cannot take a definite article. The term includes any human being.

OF GOODNESS AND BEAUTY

1. There is a limit to how much we can labor this change from *tov* to *yafeh*. It is possible that this is simply a linguistic development from the language of TaNaCH to that of the Mishnah, and that no particular significance ought to be attached to it.

   There are other instances where we detect a Rabbinical preference for *yafeh* over *tov*. Thus, for example, *Devarim Rabba* 1:1 requires that:

   שעיניו יפות הוא יברך שנאמר וטוב עין הוא יברך

   Nevertheless, the fact remains that the Mishnah's change from *tov* to *yafeh* indicates that it was the "*yafeh*" element in the *tov* which, in the eyes of the Tana'im, was significant.

2. Reference is to the idea expressed by R' Tzadok HaKohen of Lublin in his *Yisroel Kedoshim*. *Kessef*, the Hebrew for money, derives from the root *kasef*, to long for something, to crave. All other objects can be used for a variety of purposes. Money plays only one role—to enable one to acquire what one wants. Money is nothing more than tangible desire. See above in the essay entitled *Wealth*.

3. This formulation seems to argue against the opinion of Rabbeinu Tam as recorded in Tosafos Yeshanim to *Yoma* 85b.

   Herewith the background: The issue revolves about the implication when two units, x and y, are joined by the term, *im*, with. x *im* y. Which is the main unit, and which is subsidiary? Rabbeinu Tam's assumption is that the y in this statement is the main unit. Accordingly, he maintains that *yafeh Talmud Torah im derech eretz* implies that *derech eretz* is the more significant of the two, and that *Talmud Torah* is subsidiary to it. [… *de'Talmud Torah tafeil legabei derech eretz*].

It were well that your involvement in Derech Eretz [which is a given] be accompanied by studying Torah. It is only when you are occupied with both…

Needless to say, this idea sounds revolutionary—not at all what we would expect. There are those who have suggested that Rabbeinu Tam is referring only to such people who because of their circumstances have no choice and must occupy almost their entire time with working for a living. It is to these that the Mishnah is addressed. Make sure, it exhorts, that even though you are occupied mainly with *derech eretz*, that you devote some time to studying Torah.

It must, however, be admitted that the language of Rabbeinu Tam, at least as reported in the Tosafos Yeshanim, seems to require a more general application.

We may suggest the following solution. Clearly Rabbeinu Tam was aware of the many sources which make clear beyond any doubt at all that our main occupation should be the study of Torah. Thus, *Berachos* 35b: The earlier generation for whom their main occupation was the study of Torah and who regarded their labors as less important were successful in both these endeavors. Or Perek Kinyan HaTorah (*Avos* ch. 6) which lays down as one of the forty-eight ways in which Torah can be acquired as *mi'ut derech eretz*, a severely limited involvement in business activities.

So his reading cannot be interpreted as mandating a lesser involvement in Torah study than in earning a livelihood.

His meaning seems to be an approximation of Hillel's lesson to the gentile who wanted to learn all the Torah while standing on one foot (*Shabbos* 30a). Hillel told him: Do not do to others that which is hateful to you! That is the whole Torah. The rest is commentary. Go and study.

Hillel was clearly attempting to define the essence of what Torah really wants from us. What is the ultimate goal which God had in mind when He gave us the Torah? Hillel's answer was that God wished us to be good. The mitzvos of the Torah are designed to help us attain that goal.

In a similar vein, Rabbeinu Tam would say to us that God's purpose in creating man was so that he could cope with a physical world and sublimate it in God's service. [That is, of course, the underlying dynamic of the argument which Moses had with the angels when he went up to heaven to receive the Torah.] All the mitzvos, including the obligation to study Torah, are geared towards that end.

His interpretation has no bearing on the amount of time and energy that we are to spend on our various activities.

How can we resolve this problem?

It would seem that it is all a question of context. The Mishnah in *Avos* stands alone. It has no connection with what went before or what comes after. In such a situation, Rabbeinu Tam's principle is operative. ʏ is the more significant.

But *Koheles* is a megillah which has been devoted in its virtual entirety to extolling the virtues of wisdom and downgrading the this-worldly. In such a context, it goes without saying that the message is the one which *Koheles Rabba* spells out.

4. I have not been able to trace the source for this saying.

5. There is nothing more admirable than one whose bearing in the market-place is informed by those values which Torah study teaches him. Thus *Yoma* 86a: Abaya taught that *ve'ahavta es Hashem Elokecha*, you shall love Hashem your God, (*Devarim* 5:5) requires that we act in a way that will generate veneration for God's teachings.

    Thus: That a man immerse himself in Torah study and that then, when his business dealings are conducted in a refined manner, people will declare: Happy his father who taught him Torah! Happy his Rebbi who taught him Torah! See how much to be admired is the bearing of this man who studied Torah!

6. *Nedarim* 49b tells that R' Yehudah used to carry a stool to the Study Hall so that he would be able to sit in a dignified manner rather than having to crouch on the floor.

    He proclaimed: Great is labor which brings honor to those who perform it.

    The Rishonim understand this proclamation as being conditioned by the particular action which he had undertaken. Having a stool to sit on in the *Bais HaMedrash* would enhance his honor.

Maharal to *Pirkei Avos* 1:10, where Shemaya and Avtalyon exhort us to love labor, gives the proclamation a broader context.

All work ennobles. One who works for his living, brings honor to himself in much the same way that Rabbi Yehudah brought honor to himself by carrying the stool. Even as Rabbi Yehudah's purpose was to maintain his dignity in the *Bais HaMedrash*, so does any person who loves labor avoid the shame of crooked dealings and even outright robbery. Destitution leads to theft. It is as simple as that. Honest labor promotes honest living. There is no dignity greater than that.

CELEBRATING LIFE

1. We base our translation on Ramban in his sermon on *Koheles* where he points out that *vanity* in the phrase, *hevel havalim* is a verb in the *tzivui*, imperative, form: Declare *havalim* to be *hevel*.

SHADOWS UNDER THE EAVES

2. Shemini Atzeres has a dual nature. It has many characteristics which mark it as a separate holiday, but is described in the Torah as the eighth day of Succos. (See *Succah* 48a for details.) Accordingly, both the expressions which we have used, "flow into" and "culminate" are appropriate.

   The analysis which we offer in this essay can readily account for this duality. Succos, to have accomplished that which it must accomplish, must culminate in the sacred "being" of Shemini Atzeres. In that sense the two celebrations form an organic whole. However, the mode of its celebration is so radically different from that of Succos, that it merits the appurtenances of a separate holiday.

3. Shemini Atzeres is unique among all the Yomim Tovim in that it has no special mitzvah of any kind. Even Shavuos which, for us, has no tangible symbolism did, in the time of the Bais HaMikdash, have the unique Bikkurim [Shtei Halechem] sacrifice

apart from the regular mussaf which is common to all special days.

    For Shemini Atzeres there is nothing at all.

4. Within the context, this would mean that the contradictions which made the Sages want to withdraw the book are only illusory.

www.ingramcontent.com/pod-product-compliance
Lightning Source LLC
Chambersburg PA
CBHW051002060726

47593CB00017B/729